Mary Lelitia Kirkman
1801–1836

Theodore Washington Broward, Jr. ⚜ Mary Laura Call
1835–1882   1835–1920

Edwin Hollinger ⚜ Eleanora Kirkman Long
1854–1891   1854–c.1930

Edwin Kirkman Hollinger   Pope Robeson Hollinger
1887–c.1956   1889–c.1975

George Gwynn ⚜ Alice Wayne Brevard   Ephraim Mays Brevard ⚜ Elizabeth Robertson
1862–1931   1869–1892   1871–1945   1876–1961

Mary Call Collins   Sarah Darby Collins
1942–   1950–

Best Wishes—
Jane H Menton

THE GROVE

THE GROVE

For my Grandparents

THE GROVE

A FLORIDA HOME THROUGH
SEVEN GENERATIONS

By Jane Aurell Menton

Sentry Press
Tallahassee, Florida

DESIGNER: Denise Choppin

PHOTOGRAPHER: Ray Stanyard

ADVISORS: William W. Rogers, Ph.D., *Emeritus Professor of History, Florida State University*

                 Arva Moore Parks, *Historian and Author*

                 Joan Morris, *Curator, Photographic Collection, Florida State Archives*

                 Manuel León Ponce, *Architectural Historian and Professor of Interior Design,*

                         Florida State University

ART: Ron Yrabedra, Ph.D., *Artist*

                 Charles Dalton Olson, *Architectural Designer*

                 John S. Hand, *Architect*

                 Patrick Hodges, *Landscape Architect*

                 Peter Krafft, *Cartographer*

Published by
SENTRY PRESS
424 East Call Street
Tallahassee, Florida 32301

Printed and bound in the United States by Rose Printing
Company, Tallahassee, Florida.

Library of Congress
Catalog Number 98-061133
ISBN 1-889574-02-3

TABLE OF CONTENTS

FOREWORD

For as long as I can remember I have known the Collins family. I was told by my mother that we met on a spring afternoon in Tallahassee when I was just four years old. This was the year before Mary Call and LeRoy Collins moved one block from their Monroe Street home to "The Grove."

In those days the state legislature met every other year and my family moved to Tallahassee for the session. My father, Ernest R. Graham, was in the Senate representing Dade County, and LeRoy Collins, younger by almost a full generation, represented Leon County in the House of Representatives.

Although of different ages and regions of the state, LeRoy Collins and my father struck up a warm friendship that would last a lifetime. Their friendship was based on shared personal values, a common political orientation and a great love for the state of Florida.

Forty years later, while serving as Governor and as neighbors across the street from The Grove, Adele and I had our own cross generational relationship with Governor and Mrs. Collins. For eight years they were not only our neighbors, but also among our closest friends who profoundly influenced our personal life and public service.

The history of The Grove spans the years from Florida's territorial era to modern times. No other residence in our state has experienced so many events and personalities that have influenced the Florida that we know today. The long sought acquisition of The Grove as a Florida historical site, subject to the life estates of Governor and Mrs. Collins, was one of the proudest accomplishments of my Governorship.

It is fortunate for the preservation of the history of The Grove and Florida that Jane Aurell Menton, with her family's encouragement, has taken on the task of writing this biography of The Grove. I have known Jane since she was a little girl living in Miami. Her parents are long time friends and Jane is a contemporary of our daughters. She is a person of talent and dedication, who has carefully researched her subject to produce a book that is interesting, poignant, well-written and historically faithful. Of great significance is the fact that her grandmother, Mary Call Darby Collins, is The Grove's primary link to the past—as well as its inspiration for the future. In capturing her grandmother's memories and feelings, she preserves for all of us a priceless legacy.

United States Senator Bob Graham
Governor of Florida, 1979-1987

ACKNOWLEDGMENTS

The birth of a book is a complex, time consuming, and challenging process. Over five years, I have learned so much and have been helped by so many. I am especially grateful for my husband's patience and constructive involvement, my parents' unwavering support, the initial interest and on-going encouragement of Dr. Bill Rogers and Arva Moore Parks, and the endorsement and friendship of Senator and Mrs. Bob Graham. Denise Choppin was invaluable in her design work. Her artistic eye, level head, and candor were a perfect match for my evolving vision of what this book could be.

The Tallahassee area is home to many capable and creative people whose unselfish contributions of time and talent have made an important difference. All were friends before and are better friends now: Ray Stanyard, principal photographer; Ron Yrabedra, artist; Charles Olson, architectural designer; John Hand, architect and calligrapher; Patrick Hodges, landscape architect; Peter Krafft, cartographer; Manuel Ponce, my architectural mentor; and Joan Morris, whose experience and professionalism gave me confidence.

There are many others who have helped me in a variety of ways: Cristina Cola, Marjorie Dupoint, Michele Proctor, Caulley Fonvielle, Katherine Baggett, Jada Stone, Cinda Hortin, Ruthie Dickson, Tom Guilford, Mike McHargue, David Ferro, David Coles, Cindy Wise, Leslie Divoll, Bruce Chappell, and Charles Rosenberg. Mary Doug Buchanan, Charles Joiner, Carolyn Larkins, Aaron Ervin, and Gary Putnam have day-to-day involvement with The Grove, and their care for the home and grounds is particularly meaningful to my grandmother.

I thank my daughters, Jane Darby and Caroline. Though they may not know it, they have made me want to do my best.

Above all, I thank my grandmother, who has had faith in me. She inspired every word.

INTRODUCTION

From the time the first brick was laid in the mid-1820s, The Grove has held a special place in the life of one family and in the history of Florida. It has witnessed the growth of Tallahassee from a small territorial town into a progressive capital city and has seen Florida develop from a rural wilderness into a modern, dynamic state. During this time, The Grove has been both a public house and a private home. Between its sturdy walls it has experienced birth and death, success and defeat, joy and sorrow, attention and neglect. Standing resolute through struggle and triumph, The Grove is a tangible testament to civic purpose, inner strength, and family pride.

Originally secluded within 640 wooded acres, The Grove and its remaining ten acres are located on First Avenue, adjacent to the Florida Governor's Mansion, bordered by the busy thoroughfare of Monroe Street to the east, Duval Street to the west, and Third Avenue to the north. Despite the commercial development surrounding it, the grounds and home stay peacefully secluded and undisturbed. Purity of original design and careful restoration meld the past and present into a seamless pattern that stirs the imagination and punctuates The Grove's poignant and inspiring history.

RICHARD KEITH
AND
MARY CALL

When Richard Keith Call was born in Prince George County, Virginia, on October 24, 1792, Florida was largely an Indian wilderness under the flag of Spain. His road to the southern peninsula was long and difficult, but once there he became a proud and committed Floridian. Few men made a greater impact on a state than Richard Keith Call did on Florida. He played a major role in shepherding the territory into statehood and left behind a rich legacy embodied by the house known as "The Grove."

Named for his paternal uncle, a high-ranking Revolutionary War officer, Richard Keith was the fourth of six children born to William and Helen (Walker) Call.[1] His father, a land speculator, died suddenly when Richard was a young boy. The premature deaths of his oldest and youngest brothers soon followed. Left with grief, large debts, and little means of support, his mother acceded to the urging of her brothers in Kentucky (Andrew, George, David, and Wyeth Walker), packed her four remaining children and their worldly goods, and began the new century with a long and demanding trek westward.

In Kentucky, the Calls accepted the generous hospitality of their uncles' families for a year after their arrival.[2] Uncle David Walker gave them a small farm near Russellville where they lived together until 1810. Times were difficult and young

Richard learned to appreciate hard work. Reflecting on his boyhood, he remembered:

> *I learned to work, to plow, to hoe, and to do whatever else the strong hand and the stout heart of a well-grown, hardy boy could do. And this I regard as one of the best lessons of my boyhood...it gave me self-reliance and confidence in my own ability to support myself...it taught me the value of labor; it taught me to respect the honest laboring man, and above all it taught me to sympathize with honest poverty and misfortune.[3]*

Richard adored and revered his mother. He credited her with his loyal devotion to the Episcopal Church, love of classical literature, and sense of pride in his family's Revolutionary War heritage.[4] His education and the development of his character were principally the result of her guidance and example. The high standards she set for her herself and her children became the measure by which he patterned himself, and her influence strengthened him for a life that was marked by professional accomplishment and personal tragedy. Remembering his mother, the respectful son recalled:

> *From her I received my earliest and best instruction...she had a strong, vigorous intellect and knew how to impart the knowledge she had acquired....My mother, a strict Episcopalian, by her superior attainments and energy of character supplied to her children many of the advantages of a more populous country. I can never cease to cherish with admiration, gratitude, and affection her memory so long as life endures. She governed her household with a high moral power. We had no servile fear of the lash, but dreaded her displeasure. Her*

> *work and approval was the law of our government, no pleasure could tempt us and we would have suffered any penalty, have endured any pain, sooner than have violated that law. While she lived I obeyed her commandments, and had I followed her precepts through life, I should have been a greater, better, happier man.[5]*

After his mother died in August 1810, seventeen-year-old Richard viewed the future with restless uncertainty. His uncle Wyeth Walker was concerned and encouraged him to pursue a formal education. Richard studied for admission and in 1811 enrolled at Mount Pleasant Academy in Montgomery County, Tennessee.

When Indian hostility threatened the area two years later, Richard left school to join the army as a volunteer. A "slender, beardless, grenadier-looking fellow," his "soldier-like and honorable conduct" soon brought him to the attention of General Andrew Jackson.[6] Over the ensuing years, the General's friendship assumed the nature of a parental relationship and profoundly affected the life of the fatherless Call.

The following year, marching under General Jackson's command against the British in Pensacola, Lieutenant Call saw Florida for the first time. The tropical wilderness fascinated the young soldier, and his enthusiasm and military skill earned him a number of promotions. By 1818, his "daring courage" and loyalty advanced him to a position as an officer on General Jackson's personal staff.[7]

Captain Call and other staff members spent much of 1819 and 1820 near Nashville, Tennessee, where Jackson set up headquarters at his home, The Hermitage. After taking a brief retreat from military life to read law in Russellville with

This map depicts the boundaries of territorial Florida in 1827. Selected primarily because of its midpoint location between the Spanish provincial capitals of Pensacola and St. Augustine, Tallahassee became the permanent seat of Florida government in 1824. By 1827, the Calls were committed Floridians and leading citizens of the territorial capital as they began to build the handsome residence that would become known as "The Grove."

his uncle David Walker, Call rejoined General Jackson and his army colleagues and returned south to help negotiate the transfer of West Florida from Spain to the United States.[8] He aided Jackson's organization of the new territory's first provisional government at Pensacola in 1821, and became a member of the town council. Jackson, who was serving President James Monroe as the territory's first provisional governor, appointed Call to the post of Acting Secretary of West Florida until the President's appointees arrived. For an idealistic young man searching for purpose and longing for roots, the opportunity to influence the character of this old piece of America but new piece of the United States was a compelling challenge.

When Jackson completed his brief gubernatorial assignment and returned to Tennessee in October 1821, Captain Call remained in Pensacola and followed Jackson's recommendation to focus on the "improvement and development of his mind."[9] He resigned from active military duty and began preparing himself for a professional future in his adopted homeland. The political and legal issues surrounding the territorial transfer convinced him that the field of law offered a broad range of opportunities. Over the next several years, he built a legal practice and became active in territorial politics. Call's appointment to Florida's first Legislative Council in 1822 provided his first direct experience with shaping important decisions.

Richard Keith Call and Florida would grow, guide, mold, and challenge each other in the years to come. The year 1823 was particularly significant to the committed Floridian: President James Monroe appointed him brigadier general of the militia of West Florida in January (he proudly maintained the title of "General" for the rest of his life); he won acclaim for his active participation in the territory's second Legislative Council; and, at the age of thirty, he was elected the territory's delegate to the United States Congress.[10] That same year, Andrew Jackson was elected to the United States Senate from Tennessee.

In considerable part, Call's motivation to establish himself financially and gain prestige as a frontier leader was fueled by his love for a young Irish girl from Nashville named Mary Letitia Kirkman.[11] Intrigued with her since their first meeting in 1819, the enamored young officer described the slender, dark-haired Mary as having "distinguished beauty and loveliness of character."[12] Despite the intensity of their commitment, the couple faced imposing obstacles. Mary's parents strenuously objected to the relationship because they disapproved of Call's association with Andrew Jackson (a person whose financial integrity they questioned).[13] The Kirkmans had additional reservations about the "wilds of Florida" as a suitable home for their eldest daughter. Encouraged by General Jackson, Richard worked hard to dispel such misgivings but failed to gain their blessing. In a note dated November 4, 1821, Jackson tried to boost his friend's dejected confidence when he wrote: "Take her to yourself. Your industry and the aid of your friends will enable you to support her."[14]

Meanwhile, Mary dutifully governed her headstrong spirit and did her best to abide by her parent's wishes. Certain that Richard was being "cruelly wronged" by unsubstantiated rumor, she held to the hope that her parents would "in a few years understand his character and allow him at least as much merit as he deserves."[15] Expressing her anxiety in a letter to her mother dated November 7, 1821, she wrote:

As to happiness, I don't expect much as long as I remain in my present situation. I will not pretend to deny that my feelings are not changed. I am and must continue to be attached to Captain Call as long as I know him to act honorable....Still it is a satisfaction to me and a duty I owe my parents to obey them as far as I can. [16]

After four years of strained courtship, mutual devotion prevailed. Accepting the hospitality of Rachel and Andrew Jackson, Mary and Richard eloped and were married at The Hermitage on July 15, 1824. In a private ceremony performed by the Reverend Allen Campbell, "Old Hickory" gave away the young bride. One year later, Andrew Jackson would commemorate the event and his paternal affection for the couple by giving Mary a gold ring encasing a lock of his hair.

The following winter, Call took his wife to Washington for his last session in Congress. Deciding not to seek reelection, the thirty-two-year-old ex-delegate set about rebuilding his law practice and obtained the position of Receiver of Public Monies at the Federal Land Office in Florida. The Land Office was to be located in the territory's new capital of Tallahassee, so he and Mary, who was twenty-three and expecting their first child, set off to build a life together in the new territory.

When Richard and Mary Call arrived in Tallahassee in the spring of 1825, the United States territory of Florida was only four years old. The capital, once the home of the Apalachee Indians and the site of the Spanish mission San Luis, was selected because of its location approximately halfway between the former British capitals of East Florida at St. Augustine and West Florida at Pensacola. Tallahassee in 1825 was an emerging frontier village confined to one-quarter of a square mile, surrounded on all sides by a 200-foot cleared strip intended as protection from surprise Indian attack. The neighboring wilderness was so close that deer, panthers, and other wild animals were often seen within the corporate limits. Conditions were simple, but the community was taking shape. A temporary two-story log cabin capitol building, two hotels, and a general store were among the only structures in place when the Calls arrived.[17] Although development appeared sparse, lots, streets, and squares were staked out, and pioneering planter families—the Bradfords, Gambles, Chaires, and others—were beginning to settle.

Tallahassee was different by design. Unlike most other capitals, it was specifically established as a capital city. It was also the county seat for Leon County (founded as Florida's seventh county on December 29, 1824, and named for Juan Ponce de Leon, the Spanish explorer who gave the peninsula its name). The Calls became an important part of the broadcloth aristocracy that provided the territory's political, economic, and social leadership. Most of the early settlers were yeoman farmers who owned few slaves, a limited amount of land, and were largely self-sufficient. Yet the fertile land also attracted a significant number of planters from Georgia, the Carolinas, Virginia, Maryland, Tennessee, and Kentucky. As these planters bought and accumulated land, they imposed an economy based on slave labor similar to what they had known in the Upper South. They were a minority of the population but soon assumed dominant roles in Leon County and the surrounding counties.

General Call's official role as Receiver placed him in an advantageous position for land speculation. When land

These miniature portraits of young Mary Kirkman and Richard Keith Call were made near the time of their marriage in 1824. To commemorate the couple's wedding at The Hermitage, Andrew Jackson gave Mary a unique gold ring encasing a lock of his hair.

outside the city limits was put up for bid and sold at a minimum price of $1.25 per acre just weeks after he and Mary arrived, Call set his sites on a 640-acre parcel designated as Section 25 in Township 1 North, Range 1 West.[18] A man of vision, Call recognized the beautiful property's importance and knew that the land's proximity to the growing town contributed to its value. He also believed that the healthy, wooded site would be a favorable place to raise a family. Call had a small cottage built on the property as a temporary residence and set to work preparing the site and arranging for the materials and labor needed for the construction of a permanent home. In a September 1825 letter to Andrew Jackson announcing the birth of Ellen Walker Call, the proud new father declared: "We are now settled on our own place within half mile of Town, and in a short time we shall be very snugly fixed."[19]

The Calls' property was geographically and horticulturally diverse. Among its defining features were a small body of water, a large stand of pine trees, abundant walnut trees, and a grove of large live oaks set high in the southeastern corner where Richard and Mary decided to place their house. Named later by their daughters, the home became known as "The Grove."[20] To protect his family from possible Indian raids, General Call cleared the land immediately surrounding the site. The feared attack never happened. To the contrary, soon after they moved into The Grove, one of their daughter Ellen's most vivid childhood memories was of "friendly" Indians coming in from the woods to leave gifts of wild turkey at the back porch.[21]

Serving as his own architect, General Call supervised The Grove's construction. Mary inspired her husband's careful design. He wanted their home to honor her and embody the refined life-style she left behind in Nashville. Straightforward yet majestic, the floor-plan for the large house was simple. The resourceful Call overcame the primitive conditions surrounding him and literally let his land provide for the ambitious project. The majority of the building materials came from the property itself, including timbered pine and handmade brick. Slaves supplied labor. For a purposeful man not known for his patience, Call found the slow, laborious construction process to be both an education and a test of character.

Richard and Mary Call spent the next several years building their home, their family, and their reputations as participants in the development of the frontier capital. By 1831, their family included four daughters: Ellen Walker (six), Mary Rachel (three), Laura Randall (one), and newborn Mary Jane. Sadly, unnamed twin girls born in 1826 died the day after their birth. Although unfinished, the house was livable, and the Calls traded their small cottage for their comfortable new home. Richard's dream was realized: the grand house honored his wife and was enlivened by the commotion of their young family.

In the years following the Calls' arrival, the town of Tallahassee tripled to a population of more than 900. By the mid-1830s, it was the third largest town in the territory—exceeded only by St. Augustine and Pensacola—and the county boasted a growing population of nearly 6,500.[22] General Call's political, civic, and business involvements kept pace with the developing community and brought him prosperity and prominence.[23] His law practice thrived, and the success of Andrew Jackson's presidential campaign in the fall of 1828 foretold a hopeful future.

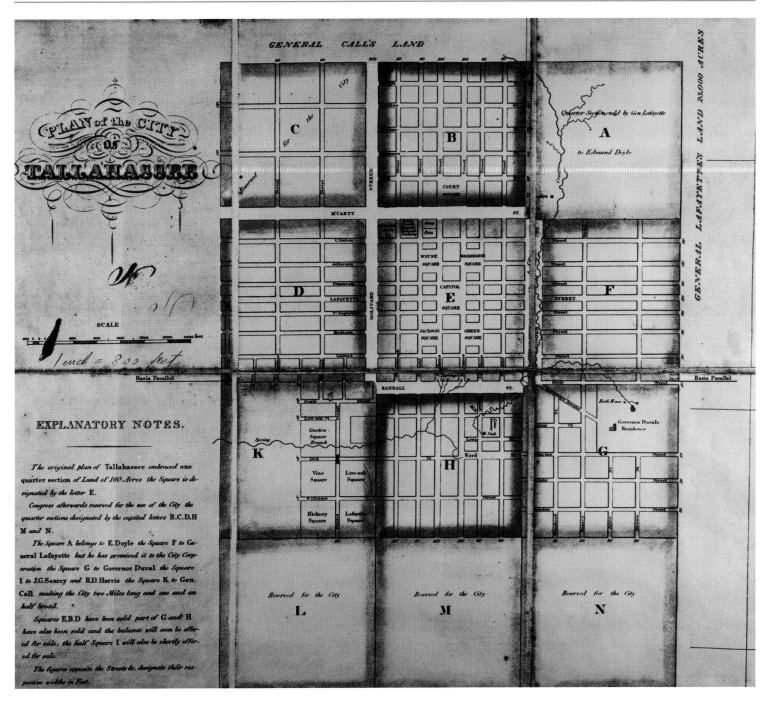

Tallahassee in 1829 was an unsophisticated but rapidly growing frontier town. Identified in this map as "General Call's Land," the original 640 acres comprising The Grove was located immediately north of the city limits.

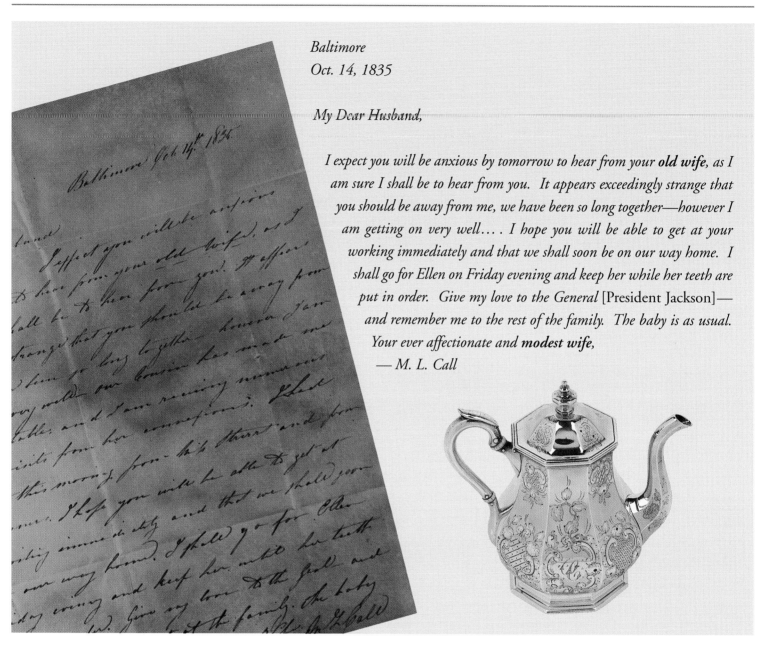

Baltimore
Oct. 14, 1835

My Dear Husband,

*I expect you will be anxious by tomorrow to hear from your **old wife**, as I am sure I shall be to hear from you. It appears exceedingly strange that you should be away from me, we have been so long together—however I am getting on very well.... I hope you will be able to get at your working immediately and that we shall soon be on our way home. I shall go for Ellen on Friday evening and keep her while her teeth are put in order. Give my love to the General [President Jackson]— and remember me to the rest of the family. The baby is as usual. Your ever affectionate and **modest wife**,*
— M. L. Call

Richard, Mary, and baby Mary Call traveled to Washington and stayed at the White House as guests of President Andrew Jackson in the fall of 1835. While Call worked, Mary took the baby to visit daughter Ellen who was attending school in nearby Baltimore. Excerpts from a letter sent by Mary to her husband during this brief separation exhibit their tender affection (*note: the emphasis punctuated in the letter is Mary Call's*). Engraved with the Call "C," the teapot is from a silver service belonging to the Calls. It was later given to Ellen at the time of her marriage to Medicus Long in 1844.

Soon after President Jackson took office, he asked Call to assist the federal government with outstanding claim disputes resulting from gifts of Florida land made by Spain before the territorial transfer.[24] In 1830, the prestigious and challenging work sent him to Havana, Cuba, on a documents search. It also took him to Washington, where the frontier lawyer frequently argued on behalf of the United States before the Supreme Court. In addition to his law practice, Land Office job, and speculative real estate ventures, General Call was also active in the establishment of St. John's Episcopal Church[25] and assumed a major role in the development of the region's first successful railroad.[26]

As the pioneer town's growing population brought in new trades and professions, the business district outgrew the confines of the main square. Expansion pushed northward along both sides of Monroe and Adams streets. Churches, schools, temperance societies, and fraternal orders such as the Masons helped soften the edges of a town where drinking, knife fights, and shootings (sometimes in the form of "civilized" violence known as duels) were common. In the midst of the growth and prosperity, The Grove emerged as a focal-point for both community and political events. Daughter Ellen had fond memories of her parents' life at The Grove:

> [At] The Old Homestead, still known as his home, for as long as his wife lived they enjoyed unalloyed happiness, dispensing a hospitality and charity worthy of their generous nature. Theirs was the Mansion House of the State, where all came sure of an earnest welcome and which all left with lighter hearts.[27]

After such a happy beginning, sadness soon came to The Grove. In August 1832, the Call's four-year-old daughter, Mary Rachel, died. The distress of her death was briefly allayed by the birth of the couple's only son, Richard Jackson, the next year. That joy was shattered during six tragic September days in 1834, when malaria cruelly claimed the lives of Laura Randall, Mary Jane, and infant Richard.

Ellen, now nine, was the sole remaining child of a once large and vibrant family. That she was spared the same fate as her sisters and baby brother left a lasting impression on her and her family. To protect their child's health, Richard and Mary made the difficult decision to remove her from hazards of the rugged frontier. They contacted relatives of Mary in Baltimore and arranged to send Ellen north to school.

In the wake of so much sadness and loss, the bereaved couple welcomed the birth of their last daughter, Mary Laura, the following January. Despite the demands of the land claim cases, Richard did his best to remain with Mary at The Grove during the months surrounding the baby's arrival. In a letter to his Washington colleague Benjamin Butler in December 1834, he wrote: "The recent afflictions, and present delicate situation of my family, would render my absence from home exceedingly painful, and unless required by necessity, should be avoided on my part."[28]

In 1835, Ellen was enrolled at a school for young ladies in Franklin, Maryland. Though close to relatives in nearby Baltimore, she missed her family and her home with increasing intensity. In what was noted by Mary to be "Ellen's first letter to her dear Mother," the child implored them to visit.[29] Ellen's wish came true that fall when her parents came to neighboring Washington and stayed at the White House as guests of President Andrew Jackson.[30] While her father tended to business at the Washington General Land Office, Ellen enjoyed a visit from her mother and new baby sister. According to a note from her mother to her father, Ellen even got her teeth "put in order."[31]

Mary wrote several letters to Richard recounting her activities with their daughters and making travel plans for their return south. In one of these letters she commented, "It appears exceedingly strange that you should be away from me, we have been so long together."[32] Her last letter to Richard before rejoining him for their trip back to Tallahassee closed with a heartfelt statement: "There is no place like home. Your ever devoted wife."[33]

In the months following the Calls' return to Tallahassee from Washington, Congress ratified a treaty calling for the "voluntary" emigration of Florida Indians to Arkansas to make way for American settlers on their way south. The treaty caused controversy and unrest among tribes in the territory, and intertribal hostility between those supporting and those opposing the emigration plan sprang into violence.[34] Led by renegade Indian chief Osceola, those opposing the plan retaliated against its supporters, and bloodshed in the territory became increasingly common. The escalating violence led President Jackson to call for military intervention. The resulting battles became known in Florida history as the Second Seminole War. Anxious to avoid a brutal and protracted war with the Indians, General Call, who retained the militia post of brigadier general, became embroiled in the conflict as he organized volunteers to fortify the regulars.

In February 1836, following the brutal December massacre of Major Francis L. Dade and his detachment of regulars near Bushnell, General Call assembled a militia and prepared to lead them to reinforce the regular troops in the region.

Gathered in St. Marks prior to sailing to Tampa Bay, Call's militia awaited his delayed arrival from Tallahassee. His wife was seriously ill, and he was reluctant to leave her. Feeling better, Mary urged him to join his men. The General went to St. Marks, but shortly before they were to sail he spotted a messenger from The Grove rowing out toward the ship in a small boat. The news was ominous. Mary was dying. Her husband's desperate 20-mile race home drove one horse to death during the journey, but he arrived too late.[35] On Sunday, February 28, 1836, thirteen months after the birth of baby Mary, Mary Kirkman Call died at The Grove. She, the first Mary Call, was buried by torch light in the family cemetery behind her beloved home and alongside her departed children. She was thirty-four-years-old. Her grieving husband wrote in his Bible:

> The home which she once adored and made happy is now gloomy and sad. She was the pride and joy of her husband's heart. In all the relations of life, she was eminently distinguished for her many virtues and propriety. She was the most devoted and affectionate Wife, the most exemplary Mother, and the kindest and best Mistress. She lived adored, she died lamented, and her memory will be cherished with the fondest and most heartfelt devotion by her affectionate and distressed husband until death shall unite them again in eternity.[36]

Devastated, Call did not return to his troops. Instead, he sent the militia on its mission under the leadership of his protege, Colonel Leigh Read, while he remained in Tallahassee contacting relatives and making arrangements for the care of his infant daughter. To John Wyse, a friend in Maryland who helped make arrangements for Ellen, he wrote:

Thank you most sincerely for your attention to my dear child. She is now almost the only object in life on which my affections are placed, and I feel the deepest solicitude with regard to her. An infant sister and herself are all that remain to me of my late promising family. My wife, my beloved and lamented wife, my only son, and three lovely little daughters I have lost in little more than three years. I have indeed been the victim of misfortune, and my days of earthly happiness are gone forever. I thank God I have fortitude enough to bear such an accumulation of evils, and while I live I shall endeavor to perform all the duties of life, although I must be a stranger to its pleasures....[37]

During his controversial courtship of Mary, Richard maintained a friendly relationship with her paternal grandmother, Barbara Kirkman, which continued during the years surrounding the premature death of Mary's father in 1826. Informing her of the death of Mary, "her inestimable granddaughter," Call wrote:

To me she was all I could have ever desired. From the hour of our union, until our separation by the cold hand of death, we enjoyed the most uninterrupted happiness save the afflictions we experienced in the loss of our dear little children. That I may be permitted to participate in their enjoyment in a future state of being shall be my continued prayer to the Almighty.[38]

Following her mother's death, Ellen remained away at school in Maryland. Only four months earlier she had enjoyed a long-anticipated, happy reunion with her mother. The ten-year-old was despondent. In a letter to her father, Ellen gave

*It was a night of darkness on the earth
The dark mists hung heavily; all nature
Seemed to mourn—and ever and anon,
The warm and sickly wind, sighed thro—the vines
That clustered round that dwelling,
Then all was hushed and still, save the low whisper,
And the timid tread.
Within that silent hall lay what remained
Of her, the beautiful,—the loved. The tyrant death
Had placed his grasping hand and claimed her
As his own;—beneath his icy touch, the beaming eye
Was dull & glazed, the tinted cheek, was pale & sunk
The form that moved, the life & pride of all that house
Was falling fast to dust.
And now they bear her out, and the torches throw
A lurid glare on all around, the giant oaks
Look gaunt and grim with outstretched limbs
Decked with the sable moss, they seemed to wave
A last adieu over her they watched for such
Long years; and the livid trees and flowers
That grew in rich luxuriance round,
Wet with the damp night air, as if bedewed
With tears;—here was her abiding place,
And now, "I am the resurrection and the life"
Broke on the silent night, and then the hollow sound,
Of earth to earth, and by that flickering light
You then might trace, the deep despair upon the brows
Of those around. The strained eye to catch one look
Of her they all had loved. And the rough cheek
Of man was wet with tears, & his firm lip quivered
With emotion, & woman's
Stifled sob & murmured prayer
Seemed her fittest eulogy.*

This poetic account of Mary Call's somber funeral by torch light was published in the *Floridian* on March 5, 1836.

a pledge she would honor the rest of her life: "I will do anything to make you happy. I shall hereafter try to obey you in everything. I feel very sorry that I ever displeased you or mother."[39]

Baby Mary was sent to Nashville to be cared for by her maternal grandmother, Ellen Kirkman, who had come to realize the depth of her son-in-law's devotion to her daughter. After years of strain and tension, Mary's untimely death forged a mutual respect between Mrs. Kirkman and Richard which endured throughout the remainder of their lives. Call later wrote of his mother-in-law: "As I know her in after years, she was the greatest of her sex: so sensible, so just, so vastly superior to any woman I ever knew, and not only so considered by me but by all who knew her...."[40]

Call wrote faithfully to his children and visited as often as possible. In a letter to his mother-in-law in January 1839, he closed with: "Kiss my dear little Mary for me and tell her Papa wishes to see her very much...."[41] With his family now gone, he found The Grove cold and cavernous and lost his passion for its completion. One month after Mary's death, President Andrew Jackson, himself a widower since the death of Rachel in 1828, appointed General Call to a three-year-term as Florida's third territorial governor.

Richard Keith Call once described himself as an arch—"strongest when bearing the heaviest weight."[42] It is hard to imagine weightier circumstances to test such fortitude than those experienced during his years as territorial governor. Following the despondent widower's appointment, the continuation of fierce Indian uprisings combined with a nationwide depression in 1837 to plunge many of Tallahassee's successful merchants and wealthy planters into financial ruin. Governor Call's frustrations with the federal government

Mrs. Ellen Kirkman, mother of Mary Call, actively participated in the upbringing of her granddaughters after their mother's premature death in 1836. Mrs. Kirkman's portrait was painted by acclaimed American artist Thomas Sully in 1817.

over the prosecution of the Indian war put him at odds with President Jackson and the succeeding Democratic administration of Martin Van Buren. Shortly after ascending to the presidency, Van Buren asked Governor Call to relinquish the gubernatorial post, citing incompatible views regarding military policy.[43] Call vehemently rejected the grounds, claiming that the dismissal was based on the President's interest in strengthening his political party in the territory.

The dismissed governor's indignation toward the Van Buren administration resulted in his active support of William Henry Harrison, the Whig candidate in the presidential election of 1840. As territorial residents, Floridians were unable to vote in the federal election. Nonetheless, Call traveled to other states and campaigned vigorously and successfully against the incumbent president. From that point forward, Richard Keith Call was associated with the Whig party, a political move that virtually guaranteed him a limited political future in the Democratic bastion of Florida. After William Henry Harrison defeated Martin Van Buren and was inaugurated in 1841, General Call's work on behalf of the new President was rewarded with another appointment as territorial governor. His tenure as the fifth territorial governor was a "reward" that would be laden with difficulty. Writing in the Apalachicola-based *Florida Journal* in March 1841, editor Horatio Waldo described Governor Call:

> *He is about 46 years of age and possesses a remarkably commanding figure and form. He is perhaps, the best natural orator in Florida. What with a fair personal appearance—a form tall and erect—a countenance open and manly—an eye, large, bright and intelligent, and a readiness of speech, with a voice of much*

melody and power, he is at all times an interesting and commanding speaker. His manners are apparently reserved and ostentatious, particularly to a stranger: but to those who know him intimately he is the affable and accomplished gentleman—the kind and enthusiastic friend; while his ardent temperament—which it may be, not frequently leads to prejudice—a natural consequence flowing from the development of strong traits of character....[44]

In 1841, a yellow fever epidemic ravaged Tallahassee, inflicting a deadly toll on ten percent of the city's 1,600 residents. Governor Call himself contracted the dreaded disease but recovered. Two years later, in three horrific hours of May 25, a devastating fire swept through the Tallahassee business district destroying nearly every building between the Capitol and Park Avenue, including Governor Call's office on Monroe Street. Though some citizens packed up their families and moved away, most stayed in Tallahassee and set about rebuilding their lives and their businesses—this time using brick instead of wood.

In 1840, Tallahassee was home to 815 whites, 786 slaves, and 15 free persons of color.[45] The area was an agricultural kingdom in the making, with nearby St. Marks and later Newport serving as Gulf ports for shipping cotton. Word of the region's beauty and expansive economic opportunities traveled northward attracting a steady mix of farmers, planters, and businessmen. Country and town became an incongruous melding of raw frontier egalitarianism and the more sophisticated lifestyles of the planters and their families. In addition, because Tallahassee was the territory's capital, politicians were always around and politics was always in the air.

Governor Call's prominent involvements and the prime location of his residence kept The Grove at the center of many public activities during the years before Florida became a state in 1845. Yet his attention to the home was halfhearted. His exhausting years as Florida's appointed territorial governor were followed by an unsuccessful bid as the Whig candidate for the newly elective office of state governor in 1845. His political defeat coincided with the personal loss suffered when his longtime friend Andrew Jackson died at The Hermitage in June. Richard Keith Call knew that his time in the political forefront was past. He turned his attention to agricultural pursuits, and spent most of his days tending to plantation property on Lake Jackson that he had acquired over the years.[46]

Richard Keith Call was in his early fifties when his gubernatorial tenure came to a close. For him, life as a Floridian was eventful and challenging—but not as he had envisioned it. The painful loss of his wife and family colored his every day. He never remarried, and he maintained a close relationship with his two daughters through persistent correspondence and visits. His daughters returned his affections and came back to him as mature young women. Ellen and young Mary Call's homecoming and the subsequent growth of their families infused their father with a renewed sense of purpose and gave meaning to his later years.

TOP: **Renowned French naturalist Comte Francis de Castelnau visited Tallahassee during Call's first term in office and artistically rendered the Florida capitol as it appeared in 1838.**
ABOVE: **The Territory of Florida adopted its first official seal in 1838. It was retained until the first Great Seal of the State of Florida was delivered to the Secretary of State late in 1846, more than a year after statehood.**

CENTER: The document commissioning Call's first gubernatorial appointment was signed by President Andrew Jackson on March 16, 1836, just two weeks after the death of Mary Call. ABOVE: Depicted here in a reverse-painted portrait on glass, Richard Keith Call lost his bid to be Florida's first elected state governor by 613 votes.

ELLEN CALL LONG

Richard and Mary Call's daughter Ellen returned to the home of her childhood in January 1843.[1] The "first white child born in Tallahassee" was now seventeen years old and welcome company to her widower "Papa."[2] Soon after Ellen's return, she met a young lawyer named Medicus A. Long. Medicus, nearly nine years her senior, began his legal career in Tennessee in 1837, at the age of twenty-one. By the time he met Ellen, he called Florida his home and practiced law with her father's cousin and business associate, George Walker. The couple married on June 20, 1844, and made their home at The Grove. During the next several years, the welcome sounds of a growing family again filled the handsome home.

The ensuing years were challenging for Ellen and largely consumed with the responsibilities, joys, and heartaches of motherhood. In 1846, one year after Florida became a state, Ellen and Medicus welcomed the birth of their first child, Richard Call Long. Another son, Hugh, was born in 1848 but did not survive infancy. Their first daughter, Mary Louisa, arrived the next year. In 1851, daughter Ellen Douglas was born. Witnessing the growth of his daughter's young family, Richard Keith Call deeded The Grove and 190 acres of surrounding property to her in October 1851 and retired to his Lake Jackson property.[3] At the age of twenty-six and the mother of three young children, Ellen Call Long took charge of The Grove.[4]

While Ellen focused her energies on the needs of her family, her husband was busy building his legal career and exploring opportunities in the political arena. In 1852, Leon County voters elected him to the Florida Senate. In a letter to their son Richard, who was attending boarding school in Elmira, New York, Ellen wrote:

Your father and myself are plodding along in an everyday sort of way. My time is principally devoted to my children and their care and instruction, only allowing so much time to society as duty seems to require. Your father is now a member of the State Senate and as a politician stands well. As a lawyer he is eminent in the state, remarkable for the clearness, energy, and promptness with which he prosecutes his profession.[5]

As a tribute to her father, Ellen and Medicus Long named their first child Richard Call.

Ellen intended for her only surviving daughter, Eleanora "Nonie" Kirkman Long, to someday inherit The Grove.

Medicus Long enjoyed public service and worked hard to expand educational opportunities in the capital area. His influential work in the Florida Senate included sponsoring the 1857 legislation that established in Tallahassee the "seminary west of the Suwannee"—the educational institution that eventually became known as Florida State University.[6]

Sadness visited The Grove in 1853 when two-year-old Ellen Douglas died. Ellen was devastated by the loss of her young daughter. A close friend who was the source of the child's middle name, wrote Ellen a letter that she would save and refer to often in the years to come. In loving children, the friend advised, "Cherish them, but be careful to love them with a chastened affection—do not let your love degenerate into idolatry. Love God supremely and them as his best gifts."[7]

The sorrow felt by Ellen and Medicus was briefly assuaged the following year when their daughter Eleanora Kirkman Long (known as "Nonie") was born. Their grief resurfaced less than two years after Nonie's birth when Mary Louisa tragically died at the age of eight. History seemed to repeat itself as, like her mother before her, only two of Ellen's children survived childhood—Richard and Nonie. The loss of her children combined with the vividly painful memories of the earlier deaths of her own siblings greatly affected Ellen and compelled the development of an inner strength that became her dominant character trait.

By 1853, Ellen's sister had returned to Tallahassee from Nashville. Now eighteen years old, Mary was a refined, quiet-natured girl with a creamy complexion and dark wavy hair—much resembling her mother. During her seventeen-year absence, the territorial town of her birth had evolved

Ellen's younger sister, Mary, attended schools in Nashville and New Orleans before returning to Tallahassee in the early 1850s.

into a bustling state capital. Finally home, Mary divided her time between her father at Lake Jackson and her sister at The Grove. After so long a separation, the family treasured her company. Like her sister, she had high principles, cosmopolitan interests, and enjoyed travel. Yet unlike the seriously purposeful, civic-minded Ellen, Mary was youthful and pursued interests that were more aesthetic and home-oriented.

After a trip to Europe in 1858 where Mary especially enjoyed the elegance of Paris, she returned to Tallahassee and married Theodore Washington Brevard, Jr., a young Tallahassee lawyer who was educated at the University of Virginia.[8] The Rev. John B. Colhoun of St. John's Episcopal Church performed the ceremony at The Grove on April 14, 1859. Soon after the wedding, the Brevards moved into a house nearby. They later moved out to Call's Lake Jackson plantation, where they lived several years before moving back "in town" to a two-story frame house located one block south of The Grove.[9] In the midst of several moves during the twelve-year period between 1860 to 1872, Theodore and Mary had eight children, five of whom survived childhood: Caroline Mays (born 1860), Richard Call (born 1861), Ellen Kirkman (born and died 1864), Mary Kirkman (born and died 1867), Jane Kirkman (born 1868, mother of Mary Call Darby Collins), Alice Hayne (born 1869), Ephraim Mays (born 1871), and Theodore Joseph (born 1873, died 1874). After she married Theodore, Mary Call Brevard was a frequent visitor but not directly associated with the stewardship of The Grove. She came to The Grove for the birth of her daughter Jane and may have been there for the births of some of her other children as well.

While the Brevards enjoyed the hope and excitement of their new marriage, the Long family's life at The Grove

In a ceremony officiated by the priest from St. John's Episcopal Church, Theodore Washington Brevard, Jr., and Mary Laura Call were married at The Grove in 1859. This teapot belongs to the silver service given to Mary as a wedding present from her widower father. Pictured in Confederate military dress, Theodore Brevard achieved the rank of brigadier general during the Civil War at the age of twenty-nine. After the war, he returned to his family in Tallahassee, resumed his legal practice, and went on to serve two terms in the Florida Senate before his untimely death in 1882 at the age of forty-six. The Brevards never lived at The Grove but raised their children in a home nearby.

was in transition. In 1859, Ellen's husband moved to San Antonio, Texas, in order to "improve his health and professional prospects."[10] Ellen and the children remained at The Grove. During his Tallahassee years, Medicus Long struggled with a lung condition that at times placed him near death. Moreover, during the mid-1850s, it became clear that he (a Democrat) held political views strongly opposed to those of his Whig father-in-law. Given his wife's uncompromising loyalty to her father, political and philosophical differences may have caused marital friction that further motivated his decision to leave.[11] In the wake of her husband's departure, Ellen faced a challenging and uncertain future.

By 1860 Tallahassee's growing population reached 1,932 in a county of 12,343 people. Leon County had the largest population in the state and enjoyed its reputation as Florida's most important farming area—strong in the production of sweet-potatoes, corn, and cotton. Within the Upper South's firmly rooted plantation system, prominent citizens like Richard Keith Call typically balanced their planting interests with those of other career pursuits such as politics, law, or medicine.[12] General Call recognized that it was time to make way for a new generation. Now in his late sixties, he arrived at a reflective phase in his life. While he still enjoyed his various agricultural and livestock ventures, Call gave his role as a grandfather increasing priority. He began to write as a way to share the lessons of his life. With the encouragement and assistance of his daughter Ellen, Call began a journal. It would be valued by subsequent generations as an instructive record of a full life.

At the brink of the Civil War, Tallahassee stirred with emotion. The debate over Florida's role in and allegiance

I am highly gratified to hear from you my dear son.... I am pleased too with the manner in which you spend your time. If you continue to apply your energies you cannot fail to learn.... What books are you reading and what progress have you made...? I am anxious that you should understand the sciences and especially mathematics. The languages are important to professional and literary gentlemen, but the sciences are important to all men in all the pursuits of life....Apply yourself, dear boy, learn all you can and spend as little idle time as possible. Time is more valuable than money, knowledge better than power. Time can make money, but money cannot buy time. I would give all I have for twenty-five years more of life, without the decline of mental and physical health and strength. With my present experience, I could accomplish many times as much as I have done or shall do in a lifetime.

A longtime proponent of education, Richard Keith Call sent these words of wisdom to his fourteen-year-old grandson, Richard Call Long, in 1860. This mahogany chair is among the few remaining pieces of furniture known to have belonged to Call.

to the Union was volatile and contentious. As the former territorial governor who convened Florida's first constitutional convention in 1838, Call took great pride in his state's membership in the Union and vocally opposed the rising tide of secessionism. He was brokenhearted when a delegation gathered at the entrance steps to The Grove in January 1861 to tell him that Florida's general assembly had voted to secede from the Union. Dispirited by the news, with great disgust and frustration he thundered from the front steps: "Well gentleman, you have just unlocked the gates to Hell, from which shall flow the curses of the damned...."[13] Despite his disappointment, General Call remained loyal to his state. He supported its efforts on behalf of the Confederacy to the point of volunteering himself for service (an offer that was not accepted). He also encouraged his namesake grandson and his son-in-law to serve in the Confederate military forces.[14]

Awaiting the inevitable carnage that would result from a bitter and divisive war caused General Call great distress. His position as a reluctant bystander was frustrating and uncomfortable. With his children now grown and independent, and the two passions of his adult life—his wife and his state—no longer sources of motivation, his health began to decline. Though the ailment to which he finally succumbed remains unknown, "bilious fever" plagued him throughout his life. Perhaps stricken by the painful and often debilitating disease one more time, the weary general became despondent and never recovered. On the stormy Sunday afternoon of September 14, 1862, Richard Keith Call died at The Grove—the home he built with such fine intentions.[15] In accordance with his wishes, he was buried beside his beloved wife in the family cemetery behind The Grove. He was seventy years old. Reflecting on the proud Floridian's life and character, historian Herbert Doherty wrote:

It was a life which had spanned some of the most important years in American history, the years from George Washington to Abraham Lincoln. It was a life passed for the most part among the people of his adopted state, Florida, to whose upbuilding and growth he contributed much....A man of strong beliefs and great courage, Call had been as tenacious in his friendships as he had been in his enmities. He was authoritarian and demanding in his own right, but he never hesitated to question authority and hurl defiance at vested power when he believed that his cause was right. A gentleman, striving to remember his obligations as well as his privileges, jealous of his reputation, chivalrous in personal conduct, possessed of the courage to fight to the end against overwhelming odds for his convictions—he was representative of a passing generation and a vanishing class.[16]

The death of her father was particularly painful for Ellen, and the remainder of her life was largely devoted to perpetuating his memory and aspirations. In the process, she became a respected Floridian in her own right. Physically and mentally, Ellen was a daughter in her father's image—strength and initiative were central to her character. As one scholarly appraiser, Margaret Louise Chapman, perceived: "They shared the same keen intellect, the same flair for self-expression, the same vitality and zest for living, the same generous and affectionate nature, and the same sin of deadly pride to the point of arrogance."[17] Ellen was a survivor and lived her life with seriousness of purpose. With a family to support and a large home and grounds to maintain,

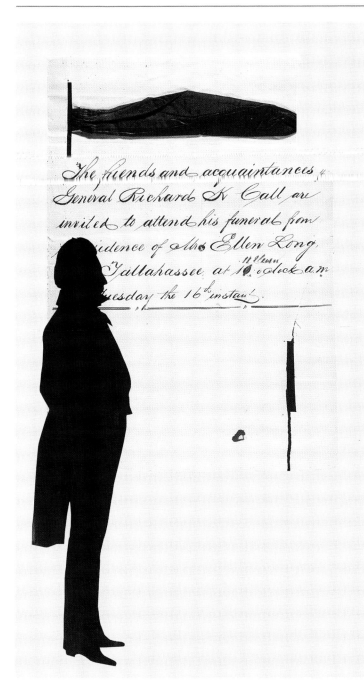

No history of Florida for the last forty-four years can be written without embracing a large portion of his, for during that time he has been in some degree, and often intimately, connected with almost everything of consequence that has concerned her....

In private life, Gen. Call bore the same exemplary character he did in public. As a husband he was romantically devoted to his wife, and through the long and dreary period of twenty-six years which have elapsed since her death, he has cherished for her memory an idolatrous love which would allow no other passion to dispute her supremacy in his heart. As a father no language can describe the tenderness of his affection. As a friend, a kinsman, a neighbor, and a master, he was a model. He dispensed his hospitalities with a baronial hand. His doors were ever open to the stranger, and the needy found a home in his house and a welcome in his heart. The widow and the orphan were his especial care. He was a humble and devout believer in the Divine truths of Christianity, and endeavored by his daily life to give evidence of the deep sincerity of his faith.

But time and space forbid us longer to dwell upon his virtues. Illustrious patriot, sage, and friend, farewell! May the future historian do justice to thy memory, and may rising generations emulate thy bright example.

Richard Keith Call, pictured in silhouette, died at The Grove on September 14, 1862. The handwritten invitation to his funeral at The Grove was trimmed in black ribbon, placed upon a silver tray, and personally delivered door to door. Call's lengthy obituary, from which these excerpts were taken, was printed in the *Florida Sentinel.*

she spent the rest of her life working to secure the well-being of her children and their heritage.

Reconstruction after the Civil War was difficult for Florida and the rest of the defeated South. The region faced a new economic system no longer dependent on slave labor. Throughout the state, many people with large properties were forced to sell or rent their homes to make ends meet. Ellen was not immune to the financial pressures and was compelled to rent portions of her home.[18] With her son Richard spending time with his father in Texas and her daughter Nonie away at school, the arrangement worked fairly well for several years because it meant someone remained in residence when Ellen was on one of her frequent sojourns. On one such absence, a well-meaning guest thought he would surprise Ellen by painting the outside brick of The Grove. She returned before the project progressed too far and quickly brought it to a halt.

Nonie, now a teenager, came home to The Grove in 1870 and was soon joined by her brother. Ellen encouraged Richard to try his hand at managing the family's property and was disappointed when he proved to be both disinterested and ineffective. Richard ultimately decided to go back and study law with his father in Texas.[19] On a subsequent visit to his mother in 1872, he met Cora Gamble. She was the daughter of one of Tallahassee's pioneer families, and the couple married on January 7, 1873. Following the ceremony, Richard returned to Texas with Cora, but she was unhappy being so far away from her relatives in Leon County. Shortly after the birth of their first child, Reinette Gamble Long, in December 1873, Cora and the baby returned to Tallahassee. Offering them a home at The Grove for as long as they needed it, Ellen sought to persuade her son to rejoin his wife and baby daughter.

Ellen's daughter Nonie was commonly presumed to be the inspiration for author Maurice Thompson's popular 1881 novel, *A Tallahassee Girl*.

The earliest known photograph of The Grove (circa 1874) shows Ellen sitting on the front porch with her son's family. Ellen's young granddaughter, Reinette (far left), would one day own the home. Note the unfinished area of white paint on the brick of the east wing (far right) of the house. Although Ellen was able to put a stop to the unsolicited work, evidence of the paint remained for over sixty years. The entry steps (far left) were moved periodically throughout the years to adjust for a progressively weakening front porch. The windowed area beneath the front porch functioned as a greenhouse for Ellen's gardening endeavors. INSET: A rare photograph of Ellen Call Long.

Richard relented and came home. His increasingly fragile health made the assistance of his mother a welcome relief to the struggling young attorney and his family.[20] In 1883, Richard Call Long, Jr. (known as "Dick") was born, and The Grove once again buzzed with youthful activity.

During the years after the Civil War, Ellen worked relentlessly on causes that furthered her father's wish to see the South restored to its "accustomed place in national life."[21] Within the lean economic climate of the postwar South, she became one of the most active and effective women of her time. A self-appointed goodwill ambassador for Florida, her involvement in the plans for celebrating the centennial of the United States in Philadelphia gave Ellen an opportunity to reconnect with northern friends from her school days. Committed to the symbolic importance of Florida's participation in the national project, her undaunted efforts earned results and admiration on the local, state, and national level. In 1874, Ellen accepted the elected position of Corresponding Secretary for the State of Florida for the Centennial Exposition, and two years later, Governor Marcellus L. Stearns appointed her to be Florida's delegate to the national event. In 1875, Ellen received the honor of being nominated by former Governor Harrison Reed for the position of the Vice-Regent for Florida on the historic Mount Vernon Ladies' Association.[22] She reluctantly declined the invitation because of competing obligations to the Centennial.

Ellen's commendable work with the national centennial celebration received meritorious attention from successive governors who rewarded her with prized posts. Governor William Bloxham appointed her to represent Florida on the Columbian Liberty Bell Committee in 1883, and she was

Dedication.

———

I DO not think that I can more appropriately dedicate this book than to the memory of my Father, RICHARD KEITH CALL, from whom in fireside talks and forest ramblings, I gathered most of the material herewith reflected; which, if I could render in his finished language and toned emphasis, would be greatly enhanced by grace and fact.

History records his work—Memory recalls his eloquence—and the fields of Tallashatchee, Talladega, Emuckfaw, Enotochopco, Pensacola, New Orleans, Withlacoochie and Washoo witness his valor; and in the vicissitudes of national progress mid passions' blaze, he plead with the North for life; and to the South in prophetic warning he told the tale at which, since, the world has paled and trembled; and while Freedom drooped he died, despairing to save. But Time has proved his disregarded word, and the honor and glory of his country is the recompense.

Yet higher still is the recollection of his moral worth, and the generous impulse of his noble heart, for they can never die in the hearts of those who knew and loved him best; and here as a grateful daughter, I render him honor.   E. C. L.

The dedication page to Ellen's literary work *Florida Breezes* (1883) underscores the reverence she felt for her father.

one of two women commissioners to represent Florida at the New Orleans World Exposition in 1884. One of her highest distinctions came when Governor Edward A. Perry appointed her as a commissioner from Florida to the Paris Exposition in 1889.[23]

During the late-1870s, Ellen developed an interest in silk culture. Converting portions of her basement as well as cottages at the rear of her home into greenhouses, she (along with several enthusiastic friends) nurtured the worms. With time, little Reinette became an able assistant to her grandmother. Ellen acquired a widely regarded expertise on the subject. She promoted her proficiency in an illustrated monograph entitled *Silk Farming in Florida* that was published in Philadelphia in 1883. After many years of work and enjoyment, Ellen and her friends culminated their unusual project by using their Grove-produced silk to make a large American flag. The women presented their handiwork to the State of Florida at the time of Governor Perry's inauguration in 1885.[24]

At the inauguration of Governor Edward A. Perry in 1885, Tallahasseeans (led by Ellen's nieces Jane and Alice Brevard, far right) presented a large American flag made of silk produced at The Grove.

THE WEEKLY FLORIDIAN
Tallahassee, August 4, 1887

A very delightful dance was given by the young gentlemen of Tallahassee, complimentary to visiting young ladies, at Mrs. Long's handsome residence, last Friday evening. The weather was clear and cool and the participants had an exceedingly pleasant time.

Among the young ladies present were Miss Maggie Pearce, Miss Jennie Brevard, Miss Alice Brevard, Miss Laura Barnes, Miss Florie Maxwell, Miss Fannie Papy, Miss Fanny Chaires, Miss Sallie Barnes, Miss Virginia Williams, and several others of Tallahassee's charming belles. Prominent among the visitors were Miss Fisher of Pensacola, Miss Meade of Kentucky, and Mr. Robert Cockrell of Jacksonville.

THE WEEKLY FLORIDIAN
Tallahassee, March 10, 1887

On last Saturday afternoon a large number of ladies and gentlemen assembled in Mrs. E. C. Long's Grove to witness a match game of lawn tennis by several of our most popular young ladies. Messrs. L. D. Ball, of Tallahassee, and J. G. Holland, of New York, were chosen umpires, and Dr. J. B. Kinney, of Philadelphia, scorer.

The game progressed nicely, while the audience manifested unbounded interest and enthusiasm in exclamations of delight and encouragement. The serving and returning was pronounced excellent by those competent to judge, each contestant displaying remarkable skill under exciting circumstances. At the conclusion Miss Letitia Breckinridge Gamble, having been successful in thirteen of the fourteen sets, was awarded the first prize, a beautiful silver nut bowl, given Dr. J. B. Kinney, of Philadelphia, and inscribed: "Ladies' Tennis Championship. Miss Letitia Breckinridge Gamble, March 5, 1887."

Miss Lizzie Cotton was accorded a prize, and each of the fair competitors received earnest expressions of congratulations from their friends. The occasion was one of genuine pleasure to those who witnessed the heroic struggle for the emblem of superior skill in playing this difficult game. Miss Gamble gracefully accepted the valuable prize and received the congratulations of an entire community.

Ellen was a generous host and enjoyed opening The Grove and its grounds for the enjoyment of family and friends. Dances and tennis matches were among the many social events reported in the local newspaper. INSET: A colorized postcard of The Grove from the early 1900s.

While Ellen was championing her causes through travel and writing, The Grove became known as "The Home of the Tallahassee Girl." Her friend Maurice Thompson, a Midwesterner and popular author of the time, visited Tallahassee during the early 1880s. It is widely believed that he modeled the heroine of his novel *A Tallahassee Girl* on Ellen's daughter Nonie.[25] Years after Nonie's marriage to businessman and future state legislator Edwin K. Hollinger in the mid-1880's, the connection between the "Tallahassee Girl" and The Grove remained in the mind of the public. The presumed association attracted the curiosity of tourists and bolstered the pride of local Tallahasseans.

Ellen Call Long was an unconventional woman in a traditional time. She did not hesitate to participate in the unusual or in what many considered to be matters reserved for men. She was consistently motivated by principle and unaffected by public opinion. From silk to secession, her interests were wide-ranging and intense. She wrote prolifically and submitted articles to newspapers, journals, and pamphlets with regularity. Some were published, but more were not. Ellen's most notable literary project came to fruition in 1883, with the publication of her historical memoir, *Florida Breezes.* The culmination of years of writing, her work is valued by historians as a primary historical source and an insightful social history of antebellum Florida. In the words of Margaret Louise Chapman, the late historian and former Librarian of the P.K. Yonge Memorial Library of Florida History at the University of Florida, *Florida Breezes* "preserve[s] a record of manners and customs, of dress and entertainment, of gossip and legend, that might otherwise be lost."[26]

Ellen's contributions to public life increased with each passing year. Remarkable for a woman of that era, she took full advantage of technological progress and wrote, published, and traveled extensively into her sixties and seventies. She led a visible life, and her home was a prominent feature of the growing Tallahassee community. Lawn tennis matches and genteel dances were common occurrences during Ellen's years at The Grove. Entertaining with a generous flair, she took pleasure in making things special for her guests. An elegant party for one of Tallahassee's newly married couples was remembered years later by the honored bride for the spectacular array of floor-to-ceiling roses that "impossibly" covered the walls of The Grove's main hall.[27] Recalling such events, the local paper noted:

> *Her home for years was the center of social life in Tallahassee; here she dispensed broad and lavish hospitality. Many distinguished persons have been entertained at the handsome old home; many brilliant gatherings, of which she was the life, have been held beneath its historic roof.*[28]

Despite her seemingly endless energy, financial strain and the dependency of her children wore on Ellen. Reflecting on her economic circumstances, Margaret Louise Chapman put things in perspective:

> *Richard Keith Call had died a well-to-do man. His considerable property had been divided between his two daughters for their lifetime, with Mary Call Brevard receiving a proportionate share in terms of what had already been deeded to Ellen. The Civil War and the subsequent collapse of the cotton market had been a blow to the Calls, as it was to most planter families. Ellen, accustomed to having money, continued to live well and to treat all her family*

Ellen's grandsons, pictured at play with a goat cart, were an active part of life at The Grove during the late 1800s.

generously long after she could afford to do so. Richard Call Long seemed not to have inherited the drive which both his mother and his grandfather had, and he also suffered from poor health, so there was no one to recoup the family fortunes. Ellen bore the burden of dealing with creditors and trying to raise money for mortgages.[29]

Over the years, pressured finances forced Ellen to sell parcels of The Grove's property to support herself and her family and to meet the obligations of maintaining the home. In 1887, her decision to sell the valuable southern portion of her property to the Tallahassee Land and Improvement Company aroused public controversy. The local newspaper juxtaposed advertisements for property within a new "attractive suburb" known as "Long Grove Addition," with letters to the editor advocating preservation of the land as a park.[30] The developers prevailed, and the undisturbed property surrounding The Grove was reduced to slightly more than thirteen acres.

In September 1891, following the premature death of her son-in-law Edwin Hollinger, Ellen incurred further financial strain when she welcomed her widowed daughter Nonie and two young grandsons, "E.K." (four) and "Robe" (two), to live at The Grove. After sharing the home with his mother, sister, and two young nephews for nearly a year, Richard Long moved his family into a newly-finished house on a parcel of The Grove's remaining property. [31]

By 1890, Ellen realized that her alternatives had all but expired. Unable to support The Grove financially, and unwilling to part with more land for fear of destroying its secluded nature, she concluded that placing The Grove under state care for official purposes would best secure its future. In 1899, she suggested to Governor Bloxham that a recommendation be made to the state legislature to purchase The Grove for Florida's executive mansion. Political timing did not favor her idea. Contemporaneous with Ellen's suggestion, an effort by some influential political figures to relocate the seat of government from Tallahassee was gaining momentum. While intrigued by her offer, Bloxham wrote her and explained his reluctance to pursue the proposal: "There are a number of places contending for the removal of the Capitol [sic], and if too much publicity was given to it by embracing it in a message it might incite strong opposition in different sections of the State and through the public press...."[32] Though she would continue promoting her idea behind the scenes until 1903, Ellen's recommendation was not pursued even after Tallahassee successfully retained the capital.

By the turn of the century, Ellen's once-plentiful resources were dry. In addition to valuable acreage, she had to sell items from The Grove in order to protect her home and heritage. It was a sad but not uncommon depletion of a family fortune. Marble fireplace surrounds, paintings, and original furniture were among the sacrifices. Of particular historical and sentimental value were a pair of inscribed limestone tablets that her father recovered from Fort San Marcos soon after the Spanish evacuated the St. Mark's outpost in 1821. General Call had placed them on the front porch of The Grove, on each side of the main door. Railroad magnate Henry Flagler purchased the stones from Ellen in 1901 and installed them at "Whitehall," his Palm Beach estate, where they remain embedded in the walls outside the entrance to the mansion's ballroom.[33]

THE WEEKLY FLORIDIAN
Tallahassee, June 9, 1887

LONG GROVE...For a Permanent Park

Mr. G. W. Saxon:

It grieves me to see that you contemplate cutting up the Long Grove into city lots. I should cry, "Woodman, spare those trees." Let me suggest to the Land and Improvement Company to retain the grove and as much more of the land as would be desirable for a park, and lay out city lots to the north of it. There would be no park in Florida to compare to it, and it would surpass the park in Savannah. It would be a great attraction to your city, and be a great inducement to visitors to remain longer in your lovely city.

Think well of it before those lovely trees are cut down. Indeed if the seventy-five acres were retained for a park, it would reward you in after years. If you can't afford it, sell it to one of the millionaires North for that purpose. It is far ahead of the grounds Flagler bought in St. Augustine.

— An Admirer of Tallahassee

By the late 1880s, strained finances forced Ellen to sell a large amount of The Grove's property to banker and real estate developer George W. Saxon. As indicated by this letter published in the *Weekly Floridian*, the development of the pristine land was controversial. A portion of the property was later donated by Saxon to the state to serve as the site for the Florida Governor's Mansion.

By late 1903, Ellen's inability to repay a series of loans resulted in a scheduled court-ordered foreclosure sale of The Grove. With her home at stake and her valued independence threatened, she acquiesced when her granddaughter Reinette's husband, New York businessman Charles Hunt, offered assistance. Believing that he planned to secure a loan for her in New York to pay off her outstanding debts, she was horrified to discover later that the transaction gave Hunt title to The Grove, which he in turn conveyed to Reinette in March 1904.[34]

Ellen wanted her daughter Nonie to have The Grove. After so many years of generous hospitality toward her son Richard and his family (in addition to her gift to them of their own home and property), Ellen was particularly pained when it seemed that he was party to the deception. The distressing turn of events broke her spirit, and her health began to fail. Ellen Call Long died at The Grove a year later, on December 17, 1905. She was eighty years old. The Rev. Dr. W.H. Carter of St. John's Episcopal Church came to The Grove to conduct her funeral service and burial. The local newspaper called it "one of the most beautiful and impressive ceremonials that has ever occurred in Tallahassee."[35]

After the death of her mother, Nonie left Tallahassee with her sons and moved to New York, then ultimately settled in Washington, D.C. She maintained a close relationship with her aunt Mary Call Brevard's family and visited them every winter, but she never returned to The Grove.

Smart, strong, independent, and proud, Ellen would have been an exceptional woman in any era. What she lacked in business sense, she made up for in character. Regretfully, the last several years of her lifelong dedication to The Grove were overshadowed by strain and family tension regarding its ownership. None-theless, time has made her legacy clear: through her determined commitment to family, community, state, and The Grove, Ellen Call Long enhanced the achievements of her father and left her own indelible contributions.

The last known picture of Ellen was taken on the front porch of The Grove shortly before her death in 1905.

THE WEEKLY TRUE DEMOCRAT
Tallahassee, December 22, 1905

EARTH TO EARTH

One of the most beautiful and impressive ceremonials that has ever occurred in Tallahassee was the burial, Monday afternoon, of Mrs. Ellen Call Long.

Mrs. Long died on Sunday, December 17th, after a protracted and at times painful illness, at the advanced age of 80 years, three months and eight days.

The day was cloudy and somber, harmonizing perfectly with the solemnity of the occasion, and a very large assemblage of Tallahassee's people, including both the older inhabitants and those who have become residents in later years, gathered to do honor to one who throughout a long and busy life had done so much to honor the State and the place of her nativity.

The funeral ceremony was conducted by Rev. Dr. W. H. Carter, rector of St. John's Episcopal Church, at the historic Call mansion and at the grave in the family burying ground.

After a short service in the spacious drawing-room, the funeral procession formed in front of the mansion…the pall-bearers being Messrs. J. B. Whitfield, B. C. Whitfield, C. B. Gwynn, W. R. Crowder, Hayward Randolph, T. B. Byrd, W. B. Knott and Sergt. D. Ellis. As a guard of honor, the following gentlemen marched beside the hearse as honorary pall-bearers: Ex-Governor W. D. Bloxham, Governor N. B. Broward, Comptroller A. C. Croom, Chief Justice R. Fenwick Taylor, Capt. R. E. Rose, Dr. W. L. Moor and Messrs. John S. Winthrop and D. B. Meginniss.

Winding slowly among the giant trees of the "Long Grove" and through the fields beyond, the mourning cortege passed to the spot where a number of the members of the family lie buried, situated in the midst of a dense bit of natural forest directly in the rear and at some distance from the dwelling. Here, by the side of her distinguished father, General Richard K. Call, and surrounded by the surviving members of her family, a few life-long friends and many others who admired and honored her in life, all that was mortal of Ellen Call Long was laid to rest. The beautiful and touching burial service of the Church was read in trembling tones by the venerable priest, and a choir…sang a number of appropriate hymns while the grave was filled.

At Ellen Call Long's funeral in December 1905, the community gathered to honor a long life well-lived.

REINETTE LONG HUNT

Ellen Call Long had taken care of The Grove for almost fifty-five years before she died and her thirty-two-year-old granddaughter, Reinette Long Hunt, assumed responsibility for the family home. The exact circumstances of Reinette's ownership were awkward and perhaps misunderstood. The truth is not clear. What is known is that family disapproval was a barrier she would never fully overcome, despite her love for The Grove.

The oldest child and only daughter of Richard and Cora (Gamble) Long, Reinette was born in Texas on December 14, 1873. Because of her grandmother's accommodating hospitality, Reinette lived most of her childhood at The Grove, where she learned about resourcefulness and responsibility as a member of a multigenerational household.

Learning was a natural part of life at The Grove, and Reinette's family provided her with an education that was both traditional and nontraditional. As a young girl, she spent much of her time helping her mother care for her younger brother, Dick. She also enjoyed, whenever possible, assisting with her grandmother's silkworm operation. In keeping with family tradition, Reinette went North for schooling during her early adolescence. There she developed an affinity for the arts and literature—cosmopolitan interests that were basic to her life for years to

The Grove showed signs of deterioration at the beginning of Reinette Long Hunt's thirty-six year tenure.

come and that formed the core of an unforgettable Bohemian personality.

In 1897, at the age of twenty-four, Reinette married a New York businessman named Charles Edwin Hunt. After their wedding, she moved with her husband to Yonkers, New York, where his commercial activities were based. Despite the distance, Reinette managed frequent visits to her family, including her two grandmothers (Ellen and Reinette Josephine Gamble) in Tallahassee.[1] Though physically demanding, the trips enabled her to be with her ailing father and to stay abreast of family matters.

The Hunts' involvement with The Grove brought them back to Tallahassee in 1903. Despite having legal title to The Grove since 1904, it was not until after her grandmother's death in 1905 that Reinette considered The Grove her own. Once ensconced as the new mistress of the house, she soon put her imaginative style and eccentric ideas to work. Reinette had a generous heart and wanted to be a person of influence in Tallahassee even as she imposed her own creative spin on the family tradition of public service and civic responsibility. One of her earliest community efforts was the May 1908 organization and founding meeting of the capital city's first, even if short-lived, country club.[2]

In 1911, after years of a strained marriage that did not produce children, Reinette received a divorce from Charles Hunt on the grounds of desertion. Though pleased to be free of her husband, she did not receive a financial settlement from the divorce and soon found herself without predictable or dependable income—only property holdings—to support herself and The Grove.[3]

With the company of her beloved dog "Diogenes," a bird named "Polly the Parrot," and the help of loyal friends David Floyd (caretaker of the estate) and Robert Aldridge (a smart, cultured, and often intoxicated handyman), Reinette applied her talents with hopes of generating an income.[4] Under her care, The Grove assumed a salon atmosphere where she offered lessons in china-painting, dancing, and poetry to local adults and children. Efforts to produce and sell a home-made tomato sauce and a unique brand of soap were largely unsuccessful, but they gave the community interesting topics for conversation.

Reinette physically resembled the grandiose personality she embodied. She was a large, heavy-set woman who wore long flowing dresses, surrounded herself with an eclectic group of friends, and enjoyed cigarettes (and an occasional cigar) while reclining on a form-fitting chaise lounge in her "studio." In her favorite spot (the downstairs southwest room), above an ever-ready easel and pallet of fresh paints, hung the life-size painting of a gypsy—a kindred spirit to its alluring owner. In describing Reinette's relationship with The Grove, LeRoy Collins, a succeeding owner, thought the home tempered her iconoclasm:

The Grove itself became, of course, an important part of her magnetism. It gave an aura of character and respectability to her views and mannerisms, no matter how they failed to conform with accepted traditions.[5]

Like her grandmother Ellen, Reinette enjoyed writing. She published several pieces, most notably the *Historical Pageant of Tallahassee*, which was enacted by a cast of over five-hundred people and presented on the front lawn of The Grove during Tallahassee's Centennial Celebration in 1924.[6]

THE WEEKLY TRUE DEMOCRAT
Tallahassee, May 1907

Mrs. Reinette Hunt has opened a class in Art at her residence. Class instruction will include drawing, painting in oils and watercolor; also a course in practical applied design and illustration. Special attention given students in China [sic] *painting with use of kiln. Mrs. Hunt has been a student of the best schools in New York City.*

During the early 1900s, Reinette taught art lessons at The Grove. The popularity of her various classes generated a small but needed income and gave Reinette a productive outlet for her creativity. Reinette's artistic abilities are apparent in this piece of hand-painted china depicting the Florida orange blossom and in her watercolor rendition of The Grove.

The bucolic spectacle was evaluated by the local paper as:

…the most satisfactory dramatic incident in the entire artistic history of Tallahassee…due in part to the pageant as written, in part to the performers and direction, but Nature itself aided in carrying out a perfect illusion *that transported the audience back to actual conditions in the forest primeval. This was by reason of staging the pageant in the grounds of The Grove where, because of trees and bushes, the various participants came in to view and disappeared as if they were in the actual forest.*[7]

The official program of Tallahassee's Centennial Celebration featured cover artwork by Reinette. As part of the town's celebration, Reinette's young cousin Mary Call Darby portrayed "Miss Dixie" in the Children's Parade.

Not surprisingly, during Reinette's tenure the land surrounding The Grove was indeed a "forest primeval." Her grandmother's desperate efforts to maintain the home had not extended to the proper care and upkeep of the surrounding acreage. Reinette could not reverse the result of years of neglect. While the natural beauty of the grounds declined over time, they managed to retain an aura of elegance reflective of the old South. Commenting on the property in 1914, a magazine article noted:

> *The grounds are enclosed by a high fence, which is covered by a tangled, rambling growth of Cherokee roses. The perfume of these countless hundreds of white blooms is wafted by the breeze for great distances. There are miles upon miles of these Cherokee roses, quantities of several kinds of honeysuckle, and masses of other flowers.*[8]

Years later, LeRoy Collins also noted the Cherokee roses in his description of the property during the late 1930s: "the grounds of The Grove were almost completely left to nature, and the briars and brambles out-dueled the Cherokee roses and honeysuckle. This gave the place an appearance of neglect and decadence."[9]

Soon after her arrival, Reinette began renting out portions of The Grove, but by the mid-1920s circumstances forced her to look more aggressively to the home itself for assistance. By partitioning the generously-sized rooms with beaver board, building a sleeping porch above the existing back porch, and adding bathrooms, she turned The Grove into a rooming house-hotel, and served as its eccentric hostess. Telephone inquiries could be made by dialing The Grove at "410-R."[10] As much as she enjoyed entertaining her guests, Reinette

The wild and beautiful Cherokee Rose continues to thrive at The Grove.

THE DAILY DEMOCRAT
Tallahassee, June 1932

"THE GROVE" SCENE [OF] LOVELY RECEPTION

Mrs. Reinette Long Hunt entertained with a reception Friday afternoon at her home, "The Grove," honoring the Prince and Princess Charles Murat.

The stately old mansion never appeared more beautiful in its setting of fine oak trees.

Footmen were in the front to receive the cars and maids were at the front doors as the guests entered.

The dining room and reception room, which open ensuite, were tastefully decorated on this occasion with spring flowers.

Mrs. Long, mother of the hostess [and] one of the oldest Tallahasseans living, received, sitting in the front parlor. She was lovely in black lace with dainty white lace collar.

Mrs. Hunt mingled with the guests and was assisted in receiving by Mrs. A. D. Hutchins and Mrs. Harry Beadle.

Mrs. H. C. Fleitman poured tea from the old Long silver service. Sandwiches, cake, mints and tea were served [to] the guests.

Those present at this delightful affair were: The honor[ed] guests, the Prince and Princess Charles Murat...Judge and Mrs. J. B. Whitfield, Mr. and Mrs. B. C. Whitfield, Senator and Mrs. W. C. Hodges, Mrs. J. J. Hodges, Mrs. E. M. Brevard, Mrs. Arthur Williams, Miss Sallie Black, Governor and Mrs. Doyle Carlton, Mrs. S. D. Chittenden, Miss Virginia P. Moore, Miss Louise Conradi, Dean Charlotte M. Beckham, Dr. Kathryn Abbey, Dr. Scott and others.

Reinette continued a tradition of hospitality when she welcomed Prince and Princess Charles Murat to The Grove in 1932.

viewed her rental activity as a temporary sacrifice to ensure the long-term preservation of her family home. The changes she made were imposed without causing any permanent structural damage, and she and Robert Aldridge saved everything (including original stone window sills) in the basement for eventual replacement.

The evening of New Year's Day 1934 threatened The Grove's existence like nothing previously. At 10:00 p.m., a fire broke out in the northwest corner of the upper deck of the back porch (the wooden addition to the original porch at the rear of the house that included a sleeping porch and bathroom). A result of faulty wiring, the fire caused considerable damage to the upper floor and roof, ruining many paintings and treasured pieces of historic furniture.[11] Had it not been for its brick construction, The Grove would have burned to the ground. The damage required thousands of dollars worth of corrective work. The original slate roof and some of the upstairs plaster ceiling had to be replaced. Fortunately, the loss was covered by insurance. Without it, Reinette would not have been able to afford the repair costs.

Several months after the fire, the living descendants of Richard Keith Call (Reinette and her cousins Jane Brevard Darby, Dr. Ephraim Brevard, and Dr. George Gwynn, Jr.) conveyed the family cemetery behind The Grove to the local Masonic lodge for caretaking. General Call had been Grand Master of Free and Accepted Masons of the State of Florida, and the local Order welcomed the opportunity to aid in the preservation of his memory. With commercial development encroaching dangerously close to The Grove, the family viewed the transaction with the Masons as the best way to protect the cemetery.[12]

HOME OF THE TALLAHASSEE GIRL

On North Adams St., just beyond the Governor's Mansion. Visitors to Tallahassee now have the privilege of enjoying the hospitality of this famous old mansion whose early splendor drew many a distinguished guest and whose charm inspired weavers of romance. For now the historic place has been opened to guests as the Grove Hotel....

When you stop at the Grove Hotel your hostess will be the great granddaughter of General Call, Mrs. Reinette Long Hunt, the present owner of the house.

To draw more visitors to The Grove, Reinette advertised in a statewide travel guide during the 1930s. The colorful cover of the publication attracted the attention of locals and tourists alike.

During the Great Depression, Reinette faced unmanageable debt. She tried a more professional approach to promoting The Grove's hotel accommodations by running descriptive advertisements in statewide publications appealing to tourists interested in an authentic Southern experience. Despite tireless efforts and good intentions, her creative business ventures failed to keep up with her home's financial demands. In 1939, she secured repayment of a loan from her cousin John W. Ford by granting him a mortgage on her home.[13] With no foreseeable means of obtaining funds, Reinette reluctantly began to consider subdividing what remained of The Grove's property.[14] Before the plan could be consummated, Reinette Long Hunt became ill and died at Johnston's Hospital on October 30, 1940, at the age of sixty-six. Though the cause of her illness remains unknown, LeRoy Collins later wrote: "I am inclined to think that in the quiet of her big house she felt the impact of what this plan of selling lots would mean in the way of destruction to the essential character of The Grove as a home…a prospect which must have forced her into a deep sense of despair."[15] Reinette was buried next to her mother and grandmother in the family cemetery behind The Grove. The estate was so impoverished at the time of her death that her grave went without a headstone until one was provided by the next owners, LeRoy and Mary Call Collins.

Reinette was a lively individual. Despite her unsuccessful business ventures, she was endearing, creative, intelligent, and resourceful. Though disappointed in marriage and without children of her own, she made a full life for herself and enriched the lives of others with her unconventional views and indisputable magnetism. Reinette Long Hunt died without the means to support The Grove, but her love for it never faltered.

THE DAILY DEMOCRAT
Tallahassee, October 31, 1940

Mrs. Long Hunt Funeral Friday
Last Member of Noted Family Dies Here

Episcopal services will be conducted for Mrs. Reinette Long Hunt, last descendant of one of Florida's earliest families, at 10:30 a.m. tomorrow in the tree-enshrined setting of The Grove, 100-year-old "home of the Tallahassee girl," on N. Adams Street.

Mrs. Hunt, 64 [sic], died at a local hospital late last night after a lingering illness.

Widow of the late Edwin C. Hunt, she was the great-granddaughter of Richard Keith Call, who served two terms as territorial governor of Florida.

The Rev. Jeffery Alfriend of St. John's Episcopal Church will officiate at services in the family home. Burial will be in the family cemetery nearby.

Mrs. Hunt had been ill for about four months and had spent the last two months in the hospital.

She was the only daughter of Mrs. Cora Gamble Long, who died Feb. 27, 1936, and of Richard Call Long, grandson of Governor Call, who served also as aide de camp to General Andrew Jackson.

Pallbearers asked to serve are: George E. Lewis, T. P. Coe, Moseley Collins, Guy Winthrop, LeRoy Collins, and Lester Wells.

Newspaper accounts of Reinette's death honored her, but failed to recognize the Brevard family's equal relationship to Richard Keith Call.

LeRoy and Mary Call Collins

While Reinette busied herself with enterprising projects during the early years of her tenure at The Grove, two young Tallahasseans who would someday live there—Mary Call Darby and Thomas LeRoy Collins—were growing-up in nearby homes.

Reinette's young cousin Mary Call was raised in the home of her namesake grandmother, Mary Call Brevard. Grandmother Brevard, a widow since the premature death of her husband in 1882, was the youngest of Richard Keith and Mary Call's two daughters. Young Mary Call was the only child of her grandmother's daughter Jane and son-in-law Tom Darby. Strongly influenced by her parents' backgrounds, her unusual childhood gave the young girl a maturity beyond her years.

Mary Call's mother, Jane (often called "Jennie"), was born at The Grove on January 11, 1868, and grew up believing that "the stork" had left her on the sill of the upstairs southeast window. She was raised in Tallahassee as one of Theodore and Mary Call Brevard's five surviving children (two sisters and a brother died in infancy). Though the Brevards never lived at The Grove, they frequently visited Ellen Call Long and her family.[1] After several moves during the Civil War years, the Brevards settled in an 1830s-era frame house located one block south of The Grove.[2]

TOP: **Richard Keith and Mary Call's granddaughter Jane Kirkman Brevard was born at The Grove in 1868.** ABOVE: **The young Brevard sisters—Alice, Caroline, and Jane—lived near The Grove and visited their Aunt Ellen regularly.**

Jane Brevard was a forty-year-old elementary school teacher when she married a fifty-one-year-old widower and former state senator from Putnam County named Thomas Arthur Darby.[3] Because he was Catholic and she Episcopalian, two ceremonies were conducted at the Brevard home on May 21, 1908—first by a Catholic priest, and then by an Episcopal priest from St. John's Church. At the time of their engagement, Tom Darby was working as a broker on Wall Street—a career change prompted by a devastating freeze that had destroyed his citrus groves in Putnam County. After a three-month business-honeymoon trip to Alaska to check on a gold mining investment, the Darbys settled into married life in New York City—a vantage point from which Tom could more effectively manage his business interests.

The birth of Mary Call on September 11, 1911, delighted Tom and Jane Darby. Having married at a point in life when most of their contemporaries were becoming grandparents, they did not expect to have children. They valued their infant daughter as a rare gift. When the harsh northern climate proved detrimental to her health, the Darbys decided not to take any risks with what they correctly assumed would be their only child. With their doctor's encouragement, mother and baby returned to the South. Tom planned to remain in New York only as long as it took to secure his family's financial future and independence.

Once back in Tallahassee, Mary Call and her mother moved into the Brevard family's large house on Monroe Street. There they lived with Mary Call Brevard (young Mary Call's "Grandmother") and Caroline Brevard (young Mary Call's "Auntie" and her mother's unmarried older sister who was a respected historian and teacher).[4] Dr. George Gwynn, Jr. (son of young Mary Call's deceased aunt, Alice Brevard Gwynn, and known

Jane and Tom Darby spent their honeymoon in Alaska before settling in New York City, where their daughter Mary Call was born in 1911. This pendant, made of ivory and gold from Alaska, was a gift from Tom Darby to his bride.

as "Uncle George" to young Mary Call, even though he was actually her first cousin), his wife Mae, and their young children moved into the house when Mary Call was about seven.[5] Within this extended family, Mary Call experienced the joys and sorrows of life and grew into a thoughtful, self-reliant, reserved, and graceful young lady.

Young Mary Call was devoted to her "Grandmother" and "Auntie." Both were active in her upbringing and helped form her character. Tragically, an influenza epidemic swept through Tallahassee in 1920 and claimed both of their lives within a three week span. The losses left a void in young Mary Call's life. Mary Call Brevard was eighty-five at the time of her death, and Caroline Brevard was fifty-nine.

Three blocks away, Mary Call's first cousin and best friend Cora Brevard lived with her parents, Dr. Ephraim and Bess Brevard, and younger brother Theodore III. Cora was only two months younger than Mary Call, and the two were as close as sisters. Inseparable, they were in school together, sang in the St. John's junior choir together, and were in and out of each other's homes every

TOP LEFT: "Grandmother" Mary Call Brevard was the youngest of Richard Keith and Mary Call's two daughters. TOP RIGHT AND BOTTOM LEFT: Pictured at the age of three, Mary Call Darby grew up amid four generations in her grandmother's home one block from The Grove. BOTTOM RIGHT: "Auntie" Caroline Brevard, an educator and historian, maintained careful family records and wrote the first textbook of Florida history used in the state's public schools.

day. The summer before they turned ten, Cora fell from a tree and broke her arm. Three days later an infection developed. The little girl died of blood poisoning on June 13, 1921. The horrible consequence of such a simple accident seemed incomprehensible to Mary Call, and the tragic loss of her closest playmate would never be forgotten.

The buoyant personality of Mary Call's father lifted her spirits in sad times, and she and her mother looked forward to his visits. He was a vivacious and affectionate man who loved to return home with unique and wonderful presents. She especially remembered gifts of beautiful dolls and a spectacular, large three-wheeler that he brought her from F.A.O. Schwartz. Tom Darby enjoyed his sojourns to Tallahassee as much as his family treasured his company. In addition to time with his wife and child, the former senator thrived on lively political debate with his capital-area friends. Their after-dinner discussions often lasted into the early hours of the morning.

In New York, the entrepreneurial Tom Darby made and lost several fortunes. In January 1923, on the eve of what he anticipated to be the business success that would enable him to return to his family permanently, Thomas Arthur Darby was found dead in his New York hotel room at the age of sixty-six. Though the newspaper reported his death to be the result of "an apparent heart attack," the cause was never determined with certainty.[6] The next day, the long-awaited date of the transaction, Senator Darby's partner hastily boarded a Europe-bound ship taking all of the proceeds with him—including Senator Darby's rightful portion. In what some considered an act of divine intervention, the man never made his destination. His ship and the money were lost at sea. Mary Call

remembered the shock of her father's death:

Father had told Mother to be expecting a telegram from him on a certain day regarding the result of a land sale that he expected to be a great success and one that would

Mary Call's father, Thomas Arthur Darby, died in New York City when she was eleven years old. He gave this engraved locket to her on her fifth birthday.

enable him to finally come home and build a house where we could all live together. For years they had been collecting furniture, china, and other things in anticipation of this day. Well, the day came for the expected telegram, but it wasn't from him but rather about him.... The news of Father's death was a horrible shock to Mother and to me.[7]

In less than three years, eleven-year-old Mary Call lost the four most influential people in her young life—with the exception of her mother. Three years later, the deaths in a six-month period of three of the Gwynns' six children (who all lived in the Monroe Street house with Mary Call)—Mary Brevard (three), an unnamed infant, and George Humphrey III (seven)—compounded the grief.[8]

Reflecting on her childhood, Mary Call said:

In spite of all that happened, I remember my childhood as a secure one. With Father mostly in New York and Uncle George gone much of the time because of the war [WWI], it was really a house full of women. We were a close knit family, very content with each other's company. With four generations living under one roof, our world was there— birth and death happened right there. Looking back, as sad as it was to lose people I loved and adored, witnessing life like that was really a rather healthy sort of thing. You lived a full life and a constructive life, and then you moved on. But, I never have liked the color black. It seemed like Mother was wearing it so much of the time—it was very depressing....I don't remember there ever being any friction. The family placed great emphasis on self-control, mutual respect, and kindness. They expected it of me and modeled it by their own behavior.... With so many

TOP: **Cora Brevard (center) and Mary Call (right) were cousins and inseparable childhood friends. Here they are pictured with Cora's brother, Theodore.** ABOVE: **Young Mary Call "reigned" as Queen of the Fairies in a Tallahassee May Day celebration. Her three-wheeler "chariot" was a gift from her father.**

different ages living together, I learned a great deal about consideration and respect—especially when it came to Grandmother. Every afternoon Mother would prepare Grandmother's Japanese tea set (which I still have), and we would have tea (I would have milk) and cookies with Grandmother. We talked about different things, but more often than not conversation would drift back to the family and to Grandmother's memories…It was an interesting home—mainly because Mother, Grandmother and Auntie were interested in so many things—travel, history, literature, politics, news. The whole family read National Geographic magazine (Auntie saved every issue in neatly stacked piles in a closet at the end of the hall), and the current issue was always on the living room table beside the Sunday edition of the New York Times with its rotogravure [picture] section. Because everyone was interested, naturally I was too.…Money was never discussed—such conversation was considered uncouth—Mother told me that we had enough for what we needed if we were careful, so I was very careful. They considered character—not money—the measure by which they and others were evaluated. I admire that emphasis and have tried to uphold that standard in my own life.… When Grandmother and Auntie died, Mother moved to the head of the table. She wore her grief with dignity and grace and expected the same of me. I think because Mother was older and was so aware of the uncertainty of life, she tried hard to train me by her example to develop traits of character that would later give me strength in my own life—to know what was right and to do it. She always said that people with character didn't buckle under— when the time came, they rose to the occasion. She expected that of herself, her family, and of me. She made me feel very loved and very special—not by being overly demonstrative, but by the way she treated me.[9]

As an only child whose father was often away on business for long periods, Mary Call enjoyed an especially close relationship with her mother. Here they are shown knitting socks for a World War I volunteer project.

Due largely to her mother's steady example, Mary Call emerged from these painful childhood experiences with remarkable poise and strength. In a letter to Mary Call's mother in 1927, Nonie Long Hollinger (her mother's first cousin who now lived in New York) commented:

> *Of course Mary Call gets her intellect from her clever Parents. Her beauty from her Grandmother. Her industry and sincerity from her Auntie [Caroline Brevard]. Her grace and adaptability from her Mother—Besides, she carries with it all her own personal charm....*[10]

Despite the sadness of her early childhood, Mary Call's teenage years at Leon High School were happy ones—and it was during these years that she first became aware of Thomas LeRoy Collins. She only knew from a distance the handsome, brown-eyed boy with wavy black hair known to his friends as "Roy." But she made a lasting impression on him. Remembering his wife as a young girl, Roy Collins later wrote:

> *This young girl with dark brown, wavy hair falling down her back to her waist, a face with large hazel eyes that were direct and steady as she talked, a nose that was distinctively straight and well-proportioned, and small dimples which appeared high over her cheekbones when she smiled, would never be lost in any crowd.*[11]

Born in Tallahassee on March 10, 1909, Roy had a much different home life than Mary Call. He grew up with his three brothers and two sisters (Marvin, Brandon, Alice, Arthur, and Sue) in a large family headed by his parents, Marvin and Mattie (Brandon) Collins. His father, a suc-cessful grocer (and avid fisherman), and his mother, a former school teacher, raised their six children under the strong influence of the Methodist church. Their upbringing emphasized respect for others, honesty, hard work, education, and the teachings of the Bible. In all of his various roles—son, brother, husband, father, friend, lawyer, public servant—these enduring values of his youth were firmly rooted and permeated every aspect of LeRoy Collins's life.

As a boy, Roy was a diligent and enthusiastic student who openly appreciated his teachers, loved learning, and had a lively sense of humor. From his teachers he developed an enjoyment and appreciation for the English language—both written and spoken. "I think now," he later recalled, "that Miss Kate Sullivan was the best grammar teacher the world has ever known—I still find continuing use for her rules."[12] His mastery of the language became an invaluable tool in his professional life as well as a lifelong outlet for his strong, creative mind.

Roy's days at Leon High School during the mid-1920s were lively but not carefree. He played the trumpet on weekends with a dance band, enjoyed drama, and was an excellent student. Well-liked by his peers, he finished his high school career in 1927 as president of the senior class. Upon completing a busy school day, the sound of the dismissal bell signaled the beginning of Roy's work day. Instead of participating in after-school sports, the industrious teenager worked at T.B. Byrd's grocery store until dark. The experience brought him face-to-face with racial injustice and opened his eyes to the plight of black citizens. Although Roy was brought up in the conservative and often bigoted atmosphere of the segregated South, he became increasingly sensitive and receptive to the cause of civil rights.

LeRoy Collins thrived in his large and active family. Pictured here with their parents, Marvin and Mattie, are Marvin, Jr., Brandon, Alice, and baby "Roy." Arthur and Mattie Sue were born later.

Happy Birthday Mr. LeRoy Collins, Attorney-at-Law. A rising young lawyer who will make his presence felt in the community. He has already taken his first political bath, and while the palms of victory did not fall on his shoulders he made a brilliant race and in doing this he has made himself many more friends by the manner in which he conducted his campaign. While he was conducting his political campaign, he was also conducting a more important one and in this he was victorious, for he won for his bride one of Tallahassee's most charming daughters, Miss Mary Call Darby. I join with all Tallahassee in wishing this sterling young barrister a very happy birthday.

LeRoy Collins and Mary Call Darby were married at St. John's Episcopal Church in a simple morning ceremony on June 29, 1932. The above birthday greeting which appeared in the local newspaper foretold a promising future for young Collins.

After high school, Roy followed his employer's advice and traveled north with his brother Marvin to enroll at the Eastman College of Business Administration in Poughkeepsie, New York.[13] After earning his business certificate in January 1928, he returned to Tallahassee and became a teller at the Exchange Bank. He also taught the men's Sunday school class at Trinity Methodist Church. In his role at the church, he came to the attention of Glenn Terrell (a man whom Roy admired greatly and who later became a respected justice of the Florida Supreme Court). Taking an interest in Roy, Terrell persuaded the earnest young man to apply for law school at his alma mater, Cumberland University in Lebanon, Tennessee. With the assistance of Collins's father who matched his earnings to help pay the tuition, Roy set off for Cumberland, where he managed his fraternity house in exchange for room and board.

In 1931, twenty-two-year-old LeRoy Collins graduated from Cumberland Law School and passed the Arkansas, Tennessee, and Florida bar exams. At this pivotal point in his life, his recently obtained law degree converged with the depth of the Great Depression and a growing interest in Mary Call Darby.

While Roy was away at law school, Mary Call had been attending Florida State College for Women. When he returned to Tallahassee in January 1931, they began spending time together in the company of their mutual high school friends. Months later, Mary Call withdrew from college in order to be at home with her mother who was ill with cancer. On an evening in early February 1932, Mary Call's mother encouraged her to go with Roy to a church social. Later that night her beloved mother died—with her daughter by her side. Jane Brevard Darby was sixty-four years old. She was buried in the Brevard family plot at the Episcopal Cemetery in Tal-lahassee. Without parents or a sibling, twenty-year-old Mary Call was on her own. Her uncle and aunt, Dr. Ephraim and Bess Brevard, offered their support, so she went three blocks down the street to live with them.

Good jobs were scarce at this time, but Roy was mo-tivated. He loved Mary Call and knew that he needed the security of a better income if they were to marry. When the elected position of Leon County Pros-ecutor opened in spring 1932, the young lawyer decided to take his first stab at politics. He told Mary Call that if he won the election they would get married. He lost the June primary by 268 votes, but Mary Call agreed to marry him anyway.[14] She later said: "If all of us who worked so hard on the campaign had been old enough to vote, he would have easily won!"[15]

Several weeks later on June 29, 1932, Mary Call Darby mar-ried Thomas LeRoy Collins at St. John's Episcopal Church in Tallahassee. For Mary Call, the event was unforgettable:

Roy and I married soon after Mother died. We were married very simply—on a Saturday morning in June at St. John's. Uncle Ephe [Dr. Ephraim Brevard] gave me away. We didn't send invitations, but some of our friends knew, and they called other friends. Mother's friends brought flowers for the altar, and Mother's close friend Maimie Lewis made a beautiful bouquet of creamy white nun lilies for me. Roy and I were both surprised when the church was filled—we just didn't expect it.[16]

With a wedding cake in the back seat, Roy and Mary Call drove to Savannah for a week-long honeymoon. Once back in Tallahassee, the young bride resumed her college classes, as her mother had hoped, and earned her degree the follow-ing spring.

Undeterred by defeat in his first political campaign, Roy found that married life motivated and inspired his legal career and his commitment to public service. Over the next years, the births of the couple's children would punctuate several of his elections. Two years after the Collinses were married, Leon County voters elected the twenty-five-year-old Democrat to the Florida House of Representatives. That same year (1934), Roy, Jr., was born. Daughter Jane Brevard was born in 1938, the year her father was elected to his third term in the Florida House. Two years later, Representative Collins became a state senator by winning the election to fill the unfinished term of William C. Hodges, who had died in office. He was reelected to the Florida Senate in 1942, the year daughter Mary Call was born.

In 1940, at a time when the Collinses' young family was ex-panding and Roy's professional career was growing, Reinette Long Hunt died, and the fate of Mary Call's ancestral home looked uncertain. For almost two years, rooms at The Grove were rented pursuant to an arrangement made by John Ford and his sister Josephine Agler of Youngstown, Ohio (Reinette's cousins). With no plans to relocate to Tallahassee, Ford and Agler ultimately decided to put the property up for sale, and the Collinses found themselves with an unexpected opportunity to purchase The Grove.

Growing up in her grandmother's house one block away from The Grove, Mary Call dreamed, but never really believed, that someday she might live in the home built by her great-grandparents. Recognizing that their chances of afford-ing the legendary old house were close to impossible, Roy and Mary Call resolved to put forth their best effort. According to Mary Call:

> The house was in terrible condition, but the idea that it might be sold outside the family and possibly commercialized worried us. Our problem was financing the purchase. We had three young children and an already strained income, but we knew that we had to try.[17]

Of this anxious time in their lives, Roy also recalled:

> We thought we could arrange this and the prospect was most exciting. Then it was learned that other Tallahasseeans were interested. Among these were Payne H. Midyette and Jack W. Simmons, both close friends, and Justice Alto Adams, who had recently come to Tallahassee for service on the State Supreme Court. All were wealthy, and this was chilling and depressing news. There would be no chance for us to match what any one of them could offer. But then, as if fate was taking a hand in the matter, when they learned of Mary Call's interest, each, in a most generous and understanding way, took the firm position that they would not offer her any competition. What a wonderful spirit![18]

In a remarkable act of providence, after more than a century, another "Mary Call" lived at The Grove. This Mary Call was thirty-one years old, the wife of a promising lawyer and state senator, and the mother of three young children: Roy, Jr. (eight), Jane Brevard (four), and Mary Call (seven months). Daughter Darby would be born eight years later in 1950. As Mary Call remembered:

After serving six years in the Florida House of Representatives, LeRoy Collins was elected to the Florida Senate in 1940, at the age of thirty-one.

The Grove, overgrown and deteriorating, became a labor of love and a life-long project for the Collinses in 1942. Note the bathroom addition off the right side of the house installed by Reinette to accommodate hotel guests—the Collinses removed it and restored the original window.

"Uncle Ephe" Brevard, a popular Tallahassee physician and Mary Call's favorite uncle, came frequently to The Grove to visit his niece and her children (Jane and "little" Mary Call are seen here).

The condition of the house was really shameful. It was in terrible shape and seemed to ache from the neglect. I had loved this house my whole life. When we realized that it could be ours, Roy and I both saw it as our opportunity and responsibility to turn it back into the family home Richard Keith Call intended it to be.[19]

The arrival of the Collins family in November 1942 brought new life and a new era to The Grove. After painting over a sign for hotel accommodations at the front entrance, the proud new owners faced a daunting task. The old house looked anything but impressive. Years of financial stress had taken its toll, and the makeshift hotel renovations added to the house's shabby appearance. The grounds were overgrown and almost beyond reclaiming. Fortunately, the house did not suffer structural damage from the beaver board partitioning, temporary electrical wiring, and plumbing additions imposed by Reinette. They were easily removed, and a good cleaning and fresh paint showed dramatic improvement. As for the rest, Mary Call and Roy viewed The Grove as their long-term project and pledged to "do what we could do when we could do it."[20]

Reinette's plan to subdivide the property surrounding The Grove left much of the encircling land in fragmented ownership when she died in 1940. Working gradually to restore the house and grounds, the Collinses spent years recovering as much of the surrounding property as possible. The Grove's current acreage reflects their efforts.

During World War II, Roy interrupted his law practice and legislative service to volunteer for duty in the United States Navy. The doors to The Grove were locked and the

COUNTER-CLOCKWISE FROM TOP LEFT: An active father who greatly enjoyed his children, Roy Collins is pictured here with Roy, Jr., in 1938, Mary Call in 1948, and with Jane in 1942. The Collinses' youngest daughter, Darby, was born in 1950 and is shown here with her mother on her christening day.

restoration project was put on hold so that the family could be together during the course of his military training. From 1944 to 1946, the Collinses lived consecutively in Princeton, New Jersey; Seattle, Washington; and Carmel, California. Reflecting on those years, Mary Call said:

These were memorable times—the fears and uncertainties of the war and what it meant to the world and to our family made us appreciate each day we had. We benefited from the travel and exposure to new places, especially the west coast. We pulled together as a family and got along remarkably well under unpredictable circumstances.[21]

The Collins family lived in Princeton, New Jersey, during the World War II years.

To the relief of Roy's wife and children, the war ended while his unit was still in training. He returned with his family to The Grove in 1946, resumed his law practice with Ausley, Collins and Truitt, and was reelected to the Florida Senate. For the next ten years, he balanced his law practice with public service. During his eighteen year career in the Florida Legislature, Collins earned many accolades. He was twice distinguished by the *St. Petersburg Times* as "Most Valuable Senator" and received the Allen Morris Award when fellow legislators voted him "Most Valuable Member of the Legislature and Most Effective Senate Debater."

In 1954 Governor Dan McCarty, a close personal friend of the Collins family, died after serving only nine months in office. In accordance with the state constitution, Senate President Charley Johns stepped in as acting governor until a statewide election could be called. Johns then sought the Democratic nomination to complete the late-governor's term. Collins decided to challenge his former senate colleague. Following two tough primaries and the first-ever statewide televised debate, the senator from Leon County emerged victorious and went on to win the governorship when his Republican opponent, Tom Watson, died before the general election. At the age of forty-six, LeRoy Collins became the thirty-third governor of Florida. At the completion of his two-year term, voters reelected him to a full four-year term by what was then the greatest margin in Florida history.[22]

After Collins assumed office on January 4, 1955, the family moved from The Grove to the Governor's Mansion—located across the street on property that was once part of Richard Keith Call's original tract.[23] Completed in 1907, the neoclassical-style Mansion was in an unsalvageable state of disrepair. Prior to the arrival of the Collins family, the state legislature had authorized the building of a new executive residence.[24] When the decision was made to locate the new Mansion on the same site as the old one, The Grove was a logical temporary residence for the Collins family. Just a few months after they moved into the Mansion, the Collinses packed again and moved back across the street. Executive offices were located in the basement, and The Grove experienced full political, social, and family use during the two years of the new Mansion's construction. After a period of more than one hundred years, The Grove was once again home to Florida's governor.

The Collinses lived briefly in the old Governor's Mansion before its demolition in 1955.

ABOVE: The morning after Collins's gubernatorial election, Mary Call and Roy "meet the press" on the front lawn of The Grove. TOP RIGHT: The new Governor and First Lady prepare for the Inaugural Day festivities. BOTTOM RIGHT: The Collins family leads a Grand March at the Inaugural Ball. From left to right are Jane, Roy, Jr., the First Lady and Governor, Darby, Murray Wadsworth (cousin), and Mary Call.

RIGHT: The Collins family moved back across the street to The Grove during the construction of the new Governor's Mansion. For nearly two years, The Grove served as Florida's official executive residence until the new Mansion was completed in 1957.

"Government cannot live by taxes alone, or by jobs alone, or even by roads alone....Government must have qualities of the spirit. Without these qualities there is no worthwhile leadership, and we grapple and grope in a moral wilderness."

—*Governor LeRoy Collins*
Inaugural Address, January 4, 1955

LeRoy Collins

Governor of Florida

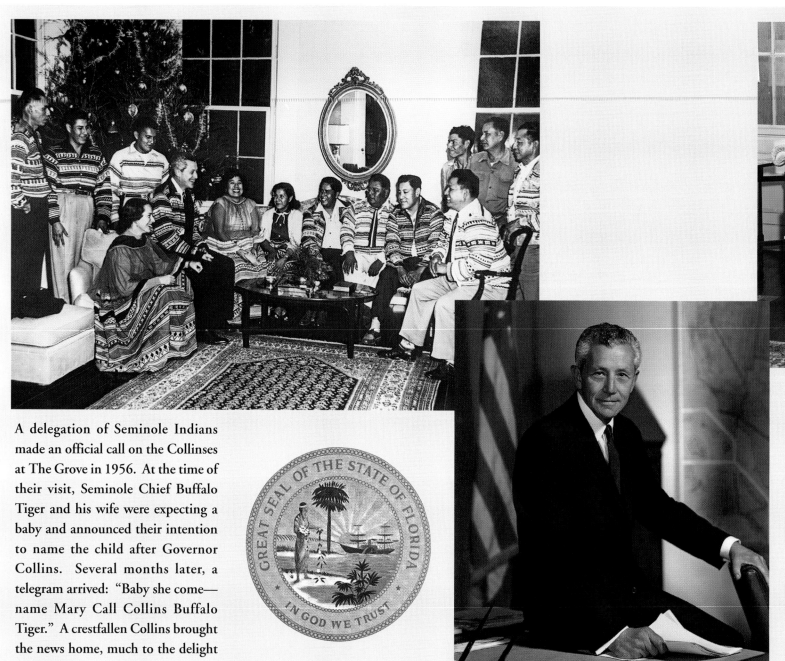

A delegation of Seminole Indians made an official call on the Collinses at The Grove in 1956. At the time of their visit, Seminole Chief Buffalo Tiger and his wife were expecting a baby and announced their intention to name the child after Governor Collins. Several months later, a telegram arrived: "Baby she come—name Mary Call Collins Buffalo Tiger." A crestfallen Collins brought the news home, much to the delight of his wife!

ABOVE: **Florida's First Lady Mary Call Collins at The Grove in her second inaugural gown.** LEFT: **As a result of his successful reelection campaign in 1956, LeRoy Collins became the first Florida Governor elected for consecutive terms.** FAR LEFT: **The State Seal as it appeared during Collins's tenure as governor.**

Pictured on the front porch of The Grove, The Duke and Duchess of Windsor came to Tallahassee in 1959. During the course of their visit to the newly completed Governor's Mansion, the Collinses took the royal couple across the street to see The Grove. Finding the front door locked, Governor Collins managed to partially open one of the old windows. As he wriggled his way through the opening, Collins recalled looking back over his shoulder to see the Duke climbing in after him, "arms and legs flailing!" The Duchess and Mrs. Collins were not as adventurous their spouses and were welcomed through the front door by the Governor and the Duke.

"This is the call of history—a history which grows impatient. Ours is the generation in which great decisions can no longer be passed to the next. We have a State to build—a South to save—a Nation to convince—and a God to serve."

—*Governor LeRoy Collins*
Inaugural Address, January 8, 1957

Mary Call's interest in historic preservation was valuable during the planning phases for the new Governor's Mansion. She was helped by her good friend Clippy Phipps (wife of Ben Phipps, an accomplished New York businessman who relocated to Tallahassee in the early 1940s). They were able to interest James Lowry Cogar, the nationally renowned preservationist and curator of Colonial Williamsburg in Virginia, to consult on the project.[25] In the process of his work with Mary Call on the Mansion, Cogar became captivated by The Grove. After work on the state's new executive residence was completed in the spring of 1957 and the Collins family moved in, Roy and Mary Call hired the talented consultant to advise them on their family home.

When Mary Call and Roy acquired The Grove in 1942, little remained of the original furniture and other household objects. In the years that followed, they were able to reclaim several pieces that Ellen and Reinette had been forced to sell. Nonetheless, it became clear that they would ultimately have to supplement the original furnishings with pieces of their own. Jim Cogar's interest and refined expertise were of great assistance to Mary Call in fulfilling her commitment to restore The Grove. In addition to Cogar's help with the selection of 18th century furnishings, fabrics, paint, and accessories appropriate to the house, long-needed structural repairs to the front porch and entrance steps were addressed with the assistance of his colleague, restoration architect Joseph Bright.[26] Richard Keith Call's original vision of directness and simplicity constantly guided their decisions. Cogar concluded his work in 1959. Because of the home's architectural and historical significance, he sought and received permission from the Collinses to open The Grove as a house museum.[27]

LeRoy Collins's time as governor was a period of significant growth and pivotal change. Highway construction, prison reform, environmental protection, educational expansion, public health improvement, industrial development, and year-round tourism were among his administration's priorities. It was a dynamic time for a state whose population soared from 2.7 million in 1950 to nearly 5 million by 1960. To accomplish his ambitious agenda, Collins surrounded himself with highly qualified people, whose talents and support enhanced his own leadership skills.

Shortly after he took office, *Time* magazine ran an eye-catching cover story about "Florida's Governor Collins," and national interest in the state's new leader began to grow.[28] In 1957, Collins was selected Chairman of the Southern Governors' Conference, and the following year was named Chairman of the National Governors' Conference, making him the first chief executive ever to hold both chairmanships simultaneously. As chairman of the National Governors' Conference, he received international attention in 1959 when he led the first-ever delegation of governors from the United States to the Soviet Union.

Enthusiasm about Governor Collins was not echoed by all. Sparked by the 1954 landmark U.S. Supreme Court decision in *Brown vs. Board of Education,* which found segregated schools unconstitutional, the late 1950s brought the nation's leaders face-to-face with issues of racial justice. These issues challenged the status-quo of the segregated South. The Supreme Court's ruling stirred heated debate and was strongly resisted in a number of southern states.[29] The issue of racial inequality commanded Collins's attention. As governor, he was constitutionally required to enforce the laws of the state. Nonetheless, through time and self-examination Collins had come to an abiding belief in "justice for all,"

and he felt morally obligated to use the opportunity of his second term to confront entrenched racial injustice. He believed that segregation was wrong and immoral, but he recognized that meaningful change would only come when acceptance of desegregation was "developed in the hearts and minds of people."[30]

Collins was steadfast in his convictions. In May 1957, the Florida Legislature confronted him with an interposition resolution which in essence denied the U.S. Supreme Court's authority to order the desegregation of public schools.[31] Nearly one hundred years earlier at The Grove, former territorial governor Richard Keith Call had voiced his strong opposition to the Florida Legislature's defiance of federal authority reflected by the secession ordinance passed in January 1861. From a new governor's mansion located steps away from The Grove, Governor LeRoy Collins expressed similar opposition to an act of federal defiance by the Florida Legislature in May 1957:

> Not only will I not condone "Interposition" as so many have sought me to do, I decry it as an evil thing, whipped up by demagogues and carried on the hot and erratic winds of passion, prejudice, and hysteria. If history judges me right this day, I want it known that I did my best to avert this blot. If I am judged wrong, then here in my own handwriting and over my signature is the proof of guilt to support my conviction.[32]

While Governor Collins continued to pursue his broad agenda for the state, the recurrent issue of racial justice was unavoidable. In March 1960, Jacksonville was on the verge of violence over the attempts by young blacks to eat at

TOP: **A 1955 *Time* magazine cover story focused national attention on Florida and its progressive governor.** ABOVE: **Darby Collins celebrates her father's fiftieth birthday in 1959.**

Governor Collins chaired the 1960 Democratic National Convention in Los Angeles. On the podium with Collins are (left to right): John F. Kennedy, Lyndon B. Johnson, Sam Rayburn, James Roosevelt, Hubert Humphrey, Adlai Stevenson, and Stuart Symington. In the row behind Collins are (left to right): Eugene McCarthy, Edmund Muskie, Mike Monroney, Hale Boggs, and Lady Bird Johnson. For his use at the Convention, Mrs. Eleanor Roosevelt presented Collins with this large gavel made of yew wood from the property of Franklin Roosevelt's childhood home, Hyde Park.

lunch counters reserved for whites. In one of his most dramatic moves, Collins went on statewide television during prime time on Sunday, March 20, 1960, with an unscripted and impassioned appeal to the public's conscience. While conceding that laws existed which allowed a store owner to make a lunch counter off-limits to blacks, he counseled: "I don't think he can square that with moral, simple justice."[33] Addressing the many Floridians who wanted to preserve a segregated society, his extemporaneous appeal added:

> *Now friends, that's not a Christian point of view. That's not a democratic point of view. That's not a realistic point of view. We can never stop Americans from hoping and praying that someday, in some way, this ideal that is embedded in our Declaration of Independence— that all men are created equal—that somehow will be a reality and not just an illusory, distant goal.*[34]

Collins's words were met with strong admiration by some and great disdain by others. Despite an atmosphere of polarized emotions, his leadership steered Florida on a course that avoided the violent confrontations common in other southern states.

Several months later, Governor Collins was elected permanent chairman of the 1960 Democratic National Convention in Los Angeles, which nominated John Fitzgerald Kennedy for President and Senator Lyndon Baines Johnson of Texas as his running mate. In the course of this lively and often turbulent week-long televised convention, the Florida governor became well-known nationally and received high praise for his evenhanded management of the landmark event.

Collins and John F. Kennedy share a happy moment after the Democratic Convention.

CLOCKWISE FROM TOP LEFT: In 1959, The Collinses' oldest child, Roy, Jr., married Jane Sisson in Tampa. The next year, daughter Jane married John Aurell at St. John's Episcopal Church in Tallahassee, followed by a reception at the Governor's Mansion. In 1962, daughter Mary Call married Palmer Proctor at St. John's, with a reception at The Grove. CENTER: Continuing family tradition, Jane and Mary Call wore their great-grandmother Brevard's seed pearls.

As his eventful tenure as governor ended, Collins took pride in his administration's accomplishments. Under his watch, Florida had become a modern state prepared for a progressive future. Former Collins aide John L. Perry characterized the governor's contributions: "No Florida governor, before or since, has had such a legislative program. He went for everything that was needed—to repair the neglect of wasted decades, to provide what was needed for the present, to lay the footing for the future."[35] The value of Collins's leadership extended beyond tangible contributions to his state. His high-minded appeal to Floridians to embrace equality brought him into the fire storm of the national civil rights movement.

At the conclusion of his governorship in 1961, professional opportunities took the Collinses away from Tallahassee for eight years. During this time, The Grove remained the family gathering place for holidays and special occasions. The former governor's first post-gubernatorial position came when he accepted the offer of the National Association of Broadcasters in Washington, D.C., to serve as the organization's president and chief spokesperson. In his new private sector role, Collins championed the public interest. He was an outspoken advocate for quality programming and a vocal critic of certain product advertising—particularly those promoting the use of cigarettes by young people.[36] His positions were often in conflict with the industry's profit-driven orientation, and he never felt completely comfortable in the job.

During the last years of Roy and Mary Call's time in the Governor's Mansion and the early years of their Washington experience, three of their four children married and began families of their own. After graduating from the Naval Academy at Annapolis in 1956, Roy, Jr., married Jane Sisson of Tampa and served in the Navy's Nuclear Submarine Service. Jane married John Aurell of Washington, D.C., in 1960 and taught school in New Haven, Connecticut, while John attended Yale Law School. Mary Call and Palmer Proctor married in 1961 and lived in Tallahassee in a cottage on the grounds of The Grove until Palmer started law school at the University of Florida. Daughter Darby stayed with her parents in their Georgetown home in Washington, where she attended the National Cathedral School and then the Madeira School.

LeRoy Collins left the Broadcasters' Association in 1964 to accept President Lyndon Johnson's personal request to direct the newly established Community Relations Service created as part of the 1964 Civil Rights Act. In the midst of a volatile time of great transition, Collins was entrusted with the task of guiding the country toward acceptance of important changes that redefined many aspects of American life. As the federal government's chief negotiator, he went to Selma, Alabama, in 1965 to diffuse tensions between Alabama law enforcement officials and civil rights marchers led by the Reverend Martin Luther King, Jr. Collins's role as mediator thrust him into a critical position in the highly publicized historic march. Following violent episodes seen on television by a worldwide audience, a peaceful resolution was achieved.

In 1966, Collins was nominated by President Johnson and confirmed by the United States Senate to the position of Under Secretary of Commerce. He resigned the following year in order to return to his home state of Florida, where he established headquarters in Tampa and

ABOVE: This 1965 photograph, later used by his political opponents, shows Collins in his role as the federal government's mediator during the historic civil rights march in Selma, Alabama. Pictured are (left to right): Reverend Andrew Young, Collins, Reverend Martin Luther King, and Coretta Scott King.

LEFT: LeRoy Collins with President Lyndon Johnson at the signing of the 1964 Civil Rights Act. At the personal request of the President, Collins became the Director of the Community Relations Service established as part of the landmark legislation.

ran for the United States Senate. He won the Democratic Party's nomination in 1968, but in a hotly-contested election, where his civil rights positions were used against him, "Liberal LeRoy" (as branded by his opponents) lost the campaign to Republican Ed Gurney. The defeat marked the end of his political career.

After the loss, President Johnson wrote Collins.

Having lost a Senate race once myself, I think I know something of the emotion you must be feeling today. But I hope you can take more than a little satisfaction in knowing that you have served your State and your Nation with great distinction and ability. No election can ever take that away from you.[37]

Collins responded:

I so deeply appreciate the message you sent me after the election. What you said was thoughtful, understanding and generous. Although deeply disappointed in my defeat, I feel no bitterness. There is a strange mood over the land. It is a time when strong reactions are stirred by emotions and by the repetition of simple phrases; a time when a label seems more important to many people than the product itself. Almost everyone who has been involved in the tough work of trying to serve the nation's needs and resolve its problems has been a casualty in one way or another. I am so fortunate with family, friends, and opportunities, and I reach for a tomorrow which seems very bright....[38]

With the controversial and divisive election behind them, Roy and Mary Call found solace by returning to their roots

During his 1956 gubernatorial campaign, when advisors suggested his outspoken comments against racial injustice were jeopardizing his reelection, Collins calmly and deliberately responded: "I don't have to be reelected. But, I do have to live with myself." Twelve years later, after Collins lost his bid for the United States Senate in a campaign fraught with racial undertones, he was disheartened but never doubted the correctness of his positions: "I was deeply disappointed, but I was proud of what I did to advance civil rights. If I had just remained silent and not done what I did, I would have forsaken what I strongly believed to be right, and that would have been hard for me to live with."[39]

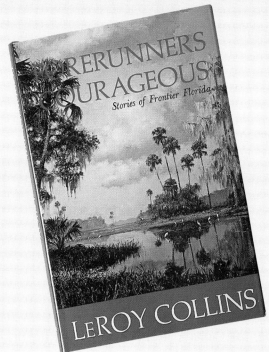

ABOVE AND TOP LEFT: Collins toasts his wife in celebration of their fiftieth wedding anniversary in 1982. Here they are surrounded by their grandchildren, who gathered for the happy occasion. LEFT: Collins's book, *Forerunners Courageous*, was written in 1971. The cover featured artwork by painter A. E. Backus.

and their home. Since daughter Darby was a student at Randolph Macon Woman's College in Virginia, they were unaccompanied in their move back to The Grove. Collins joined the Ervin Varn law firm in Tallahassee. He also began to pursue two long-held goals—to build a cottage on Dog Island (a small, remote barrier island off of Florida's Gulf Coast) and to write. His unsuccessful Senate campaign left him with considerable debt. At the urging of Nelson Poynter of the *St. Petersburg Times*, Collins took weekend retreats to Dog Island and wrote the stories and poetry of frontier Florida that were published in 1971 under the title *Forerunners Courageous*. The book sold well and enabled him to pay off his campaign debt.

L eRoy Collins never fully retired from public or professional life. He maintained his law practice, wrote weekly columns for the *St. Petersburg Times*, and actively served on various boards and commissions throughout the remainder of his life. In 1989, an x-ray following a routine shoulder operation revealed a metastasized malignancy in his lung. With the constant support of his family, he began a difficult series of treatments. On his good days he maintained a schedule at his law office, and for as long as his health allowed he took weekend trips with his family to his beloved Dog Island. He also participated in the making of a film documentary about his career entitled *Where He Stood* and continued to serve as a contributing member of the Board of Directors for the Collins Center for Public Policy (a statewide, nonpartisan public policy institute named in his honor).

Similar to his political forebear Richard Keith Call, LeRoy Collins devoted the prime of his political life to controversial and unpopular stands—with public service his inspiration and devotion. Unlike General Call, Governor Collins lived to see

A small cottage on Dog Island, a barrier island off Florida's west coast, was Collins's favorite retreat and a site for many happy times with his family and friends.

time vindicate his efforts and history recognize him as a leader and a statesman. Among the numerous awards and distinctions bestowed upon him, Collins was the first recipient of the ACLU Foundation of Florida's "Nelson Poynter Award" in 1978 and was the first person honored with the "Great Floridian" award in 1981.

Continuing the tradition of the first Mary Call, Mary Call Collins was a constant partner and confidant in her husband's endeavors, offering encouragement and counsel in all aspects of his life and career. On the afternoon of March 12, 1991, LeRoy Collins died at The Grove, two days after his eighty-second birthday. He was buried in the family cemetery behind The Grove—only a few feet from the burial place of Richard Keith Call.

In the years after LeRoy and Mary Call Collins returned to Tallahassee, The Grove again enjoyed its intended role as a family gathering place for children, grandchildren, great-grandchildren, and friends. The home became the traditional spot for birthdays, anniversaries, picnics, weddings, and gatherings after church services at St. John's. Tricycles, bicycles, and tree swings reflected the continuous activity.

Six years before his death, LeRoy and Mary Call (with their four children), made the careful and difficult decision to sell The Grove to the State of Florida for eventual use as a house museum. Terms of the sale included a lease agreement that enabled them to remain in their home for the remainder of their lives. Since the death of her husband in March 1991, Mary Call Collins—the adored matriarch of her four children and their spouses, twelve grandchildren, and twelve great-grandchildren—has continued to pursue activities that emphasize a family-centered life in the home of her ancestors.

For most of the time during LeRoy and Mary Call Collins's stewardship of The Grove, their experiences and memories have been happy ones. In startling contrast to the sad memories of Richard Keith Call's family, good health, strong children, and long lives have sustained the Collins years. Their home thrives as an island of peace and tranquillity—set apart from the fast-paced world surrounding it. Weathering a history of struggle and triumph, The Grove remains a monument and a symbol that Floridians can look upon with pride and inspiration.

But Call's story…becomes more than the story of his own life and the lives of his descendants. It becomes the story of a beautiful and strongly built house….This, then, may be regarded in the end as the true love story of a house, a tiny star in the civilization of its time.

LeRoy Collins, *Forerunners Courageous*

OPPOSITE: **LeRoy and Mary Call Collins at The Grove in 1980.**

ABOVE: Roy and Mary Call's youngest daughter, Darby, married Fred Begeman on the front steps of The Grove in 1973. Following ceremonies at St. John's Church, two Collins granddaughters had wedding receptions at The Grove. TOP RIGHT: Jane Brevard Aurell married Stephen Menton in the fall of 1991 and celebrated with a candlelight evening reception. RIGHT: Mary Call Proctor married Molitor Ford in 1993 and celebrated their wedding day with a spring garden party reception.

ABOVE: Easter egg hunts at The Grove are special occasions for the seventh generation.

RIGHT: Four generations at The Grove. Clockwise from center are Mary Call Collins, Mary Call Proctor, Roy Molitor Ford III, Proctor Kirkman Ford, Mary Call Ford, Caroline Brevard Menton, Jane Aurell Menton, Jane Darby Menton, and Jane Collins Aurell (1998).

THE ARCHITECTURE

"There is a dignity in its simplicity. It's not fancy, but direct."
—MARY CALL COLLINS

Carved from the frontier landscape during the first decade after Florida became a territory in 1824, The Grove stands as an architectural example of rustic refinement. Although never completely finished, the historic home is the remarkably resourceful accomplishment of unskilled labor working with indigenous materials under primitive conditions.

When Richard Keith and Mary Call acquired their 640-acre section of land (Section 25, Township 1 North, Range 1 West) in May 1825, they sited their home among a cluster of moss-hung oak trees on a hill of 204 feet—one of Tallahassee's highest locales.[1] Like other gentleman-builders of the time,

the ambitious frontiersman served as his own architect and likely collected his ideas from pattern books and images recalled from his earlier exposure to the stately homes of Virginia, Kentucky, and Tennessee. Consistent with his personality, the home built to honor his wife is strong and direct, conveying a timelessness and dignity in the chaste simplicity of its Grecian lines.

Announced by a grand temple-front portico, The Grove expresses the early Greek Revival style with its emphasis on balance, symmetry, and proportion. A wide pedimented gable with flushed siding extends over the expansive front porch and is supported by four large, round, solid columns made

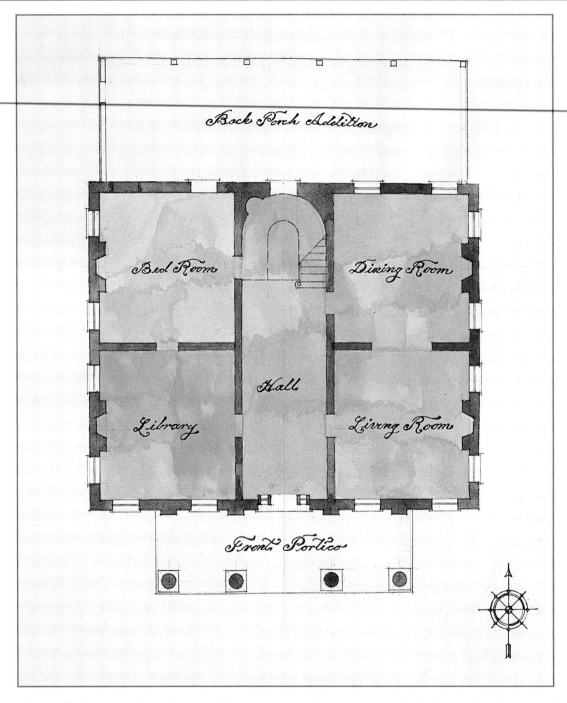

Back Porch Addition

Bed Room

Dining Room

Hall

Library

Living Room

Front Portico

This floor plan rendering of The Grove by architectural designer Charles D. Olson represents the original design of the first floor and incorporates the back porch addition made by the Collinses in 1952. The second floor repeats the plan.

of hand-crafted curved brick. Four pilasters repeat the columns and, with the exception of the plain interior pilasters closest to the entry doors, are similarly adorned with Doric entablature. The interior pilasters lack capitals in order not to interfere with the line of the upper-story windows. Consistent with the Grecian style, all walls, columns, and pilasters of the portico are covered with stucco and painted white—the result provides a visual contrast to the red brick of the home's entirety. The large double-hung windows are impressive with six-over-six light configurations and stone sills.

Stylistically, the main entry to the home—stacked double doors with side lights and elliptical fan lights—is Federal. Such entries were popular from the 1790s to about 1830.[2] Wood blocks remain where capitals were originally intended for the fluted columns framing the entry doors. In yet another unfinished detail, protruding wall brackets indicate where a wrought-iron balcony was planned. Ordered from England, family lore maintains that the piece was lost at sea in route to Florida and was never reordered. Following the death of his beloved wife, Call lost his passion for the home. Ellen Call Long never attempted to complete the unfinished details left by her father. Perhaps she believed that to do so would have intruded upon the memory of her mother. Subsequent members of the family who have owned The Grove—Reinette Long Hunt and Mary Call Darby Collins—continued the tradition, recognizing that to "finish" the house would destroy the family history made vivid by the architectural fabric.

The original wooden entrance stairs leading up to the portico have been replaced several times over the years due to rotting and structural decay. Designed by restoration architect Joseph Elliot Bright, the current Federal-style entrance steps were added in 1959 to harmonize with the fanned elements of the front doors.[3]

The interior and exterior walls of the house are made of brick that was dug, molded, and fired on the property.[4] Load-bearing walls taper upward three stories from their thickest width of nearly two feet at the basement level. A direct application of plaster covers the walls of the interior. Aside from the front portico area of stucco-covered brick, the majority of the exterior brickwork is exposed. The bricks are arranged in Garden Style bond, which would have been the easiest and strongest bonding configuration for unskilled laborers during the time of construction.

With the exception of the windows (which were probably ordered), the majority of wood used in the house was timbered on the property and hand-tooled. The wide heart-pine floorboards used throughout the first and second stories and the massive floor joists exposed in the basement reveal the magnitude of the job.

Consisting of two stacked floors atop a raised basement, the house is crowned by a hipped roof cornered with four working chimneys. Each block of the encircling exterior dentil cornice is hand-carved and individual in placement.

The floor plan of The Grove is Georgian—simple, traditional, and functionally designed. No permanent changes to the home's basic body have been made through time. On the main floor, double entrance doors open into a broad central hall that is thirteen feet across and flanked on each side by two large rooms measuring twenty feet wide by twenty-two feet deep. Originally designed to encourage comfortable air flow during the warm season, the ceilings are slightly over twelve feet high, and the wide central hall connects the front doorway to another equally broad doorway at the rear. Each room has four large windows (though the rooms at the north end of the house no longer have the north facing windows because of a back porch improvement made in 1952). Intended for the provision of heat in the winter months, each room contains a working fireplace.

The interior architecture is plain but handsome. All of the downstairs rooms have wide baseboards but no crown moulding. The doors are hand-planed and still have the original hardware. Modern electricity runs through the baseboards to lamps—there are no switches on the walls. In 1955, central air conditioning for the first floor and basement was installed.[5]

The two rooms on the east side of the main floor are the most ornate, with doors and windows adorned with Grecian peak cornices. The fireplaces in these rooms retain their original marble mantles and surrounds. Unlike the other rooms of the house, these rooms are connected by massive hand-planed pocket doors. Across the hall, the rooms on the west side of the house have simple, squared-off door and window casings. The fireplaces have wooden shelf mantles that repeat the simplicity of the moulding but lack the original marble surrounds—they were sold during Ellen Call Long's tenure to defray the costs of living at The Grove.

A graceful cantilevered staircase (said to be inspired by the staircase at The Hermitage) with a mahogany handrail connects the first and second floors. The floor plan of the upper story repeats that of the main floor, but the ceilings are six

inches higher. The two adjoining rooms on each side of the upstairs hall have wide floorboards, simple chair railing, and crown moulding. The casings for the windows and doors are of the Greek Revival corner-block style. The palmette motif seen within the casing "blocks" of the southwest room was probably intended for all rooms, or perhaps only used to distinguish the master bedroom.

Folding doors and panel infills at the base of the main stairway screen a narrow passageway of uneven steps leading to the basement. Scaffolding marks can still be seen in the brick walls of the stairwell. The floor plan of the basement mimics that of the upper stories. The ceiling is significantly lower and reveals the amazing amount of handwork employed to create the floor system. Over the years, the original dirt floor of the basement has been fortified, and a cistern (originally intended as a source of water in the event of Indian attack) in the southwest corner has been removed. Another cistern, located just beyond the back porch addition is now hidden beneath a bed of ivy.

The original wooden porch attached to the back of the house was enlarged by Reinette Long Hunt in the 1920s and ultimately replaced with an enclosed two-story addition contributed by the Collins family in 1952. Architect David Biers carefully designed the improvement to enable the modern conveniences of plumbing and kitchen needs without detracting from the scale and symmetry of the house.[6]

The home's architectural significance was recognized in 1972, when The Grove was listed on the National Register of Historic Places. The following year the property was zoned Historic-Cultural by the City of Tallahassee.

A broad entrance hall extends the length of the main floor and is flanked by two rooms on each side. The heart pine floors are original and were made of wood from the property. With twin niches nearly seven feet tall complementing its graceful proportions, the staircase was reputedly inspired by the one at The Hermitage.

BELOW AND LEFT: The living room and dining room were originally intended as the main reception areas of the house and are connected by massive pocket doors. The trim work in these rooms was hand-tooled and appears more formal than the rather simple woodwork evident in other rooms. Portraits of Richard Keith Call (a reproduction of the original located in the Florida Capitol) and of his daughter Mary Call Brevard hang above the marble mantles. The collection of furniture in these rooms and throughout The Grove is predominately eighteenth century.

The library stands across the hall from the living room and is plain in moulding detail.

Through folding doors opening beneath the main stairwell, a narrow passage of uneven steps leads into the basement.

Scaffolding marks remain in the walls of this simple passageway.

Now equipped with electrical appliances, the raised basement continues to house a kitchen and informal dining area as it did in territorial times. The low, exposed ceiling in the dining area reveals hand-tooled beams that evidence the demanding manual labor involved in building The Grove. This copper pot belonged to the Calls and is original to the house.

LeRoy Collins's office in the basement was established during his time as governor and remained a comfortable refuge for work and relaxation throughout his life. His well-worn desk (at the left of the photograph) was previously used by the builder of The Grove, Richard Keith Call.

With slightly higher ceilings, the upstairs hall repeats the basic proportions of the downstairs and is flanked by four bedrooms.

In 1952, the inconveniences of a basement kitchen and inadequate bathrooms for a family of six were alleviated with a two-story addition across the rear of the house where a back porch had previously existed. Enclosed with triple-hung windows, this space provided the main floor with a small modern kitchen, a bathroom, and a large sun porch. Two large bathrooms separated by a nursery were gained upstairs. The addition was carefully balanced and scaled to Call's original design.

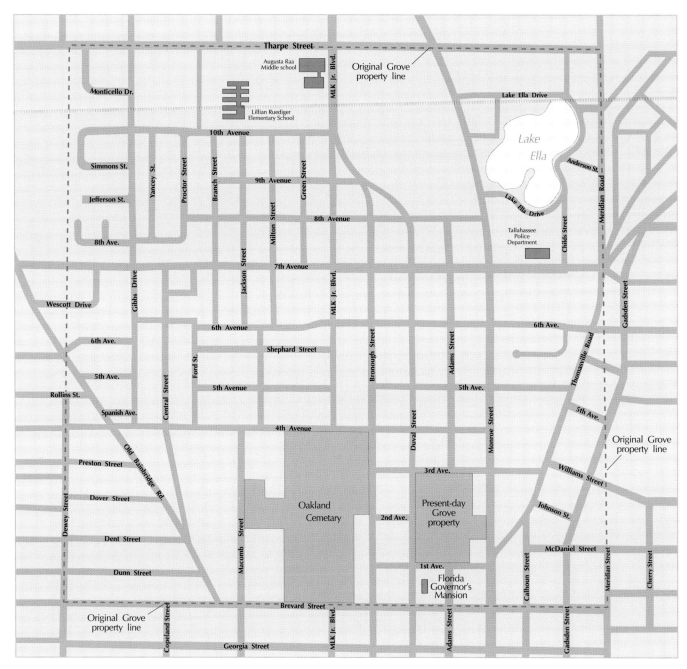

Within the context of modern Tallahassee, this map relates the current boundaries of The Grove and its grounds to Richard Keith Call's original 640 acre tract of land. This view was digitally rendered by cartographer Peter Krafft (1998). Since the Calls arrived in 1825, Florida's capital at Tallahassee has grown from an emerging village of 300 into a thriving city of 227,000.[7]

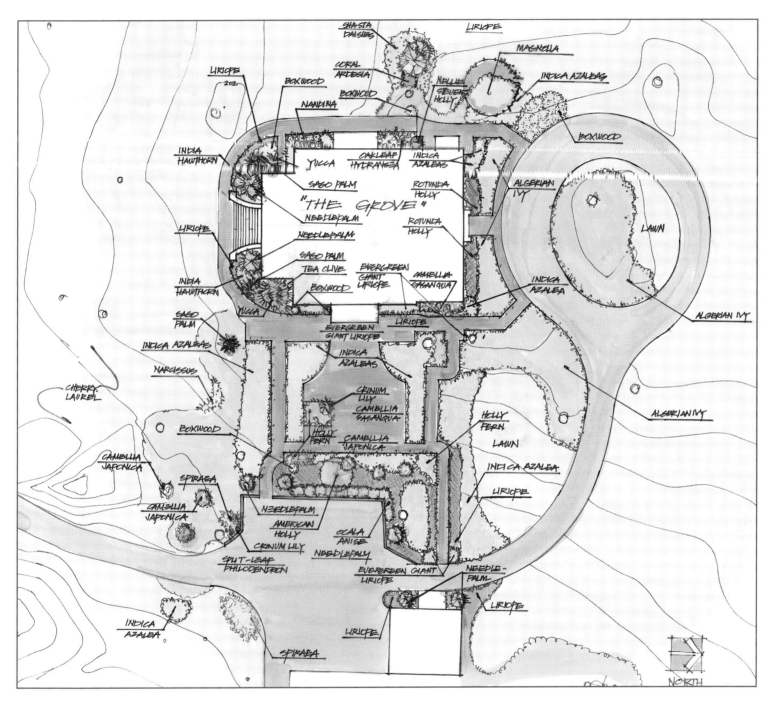

Landscape architect Patrick Hodges prepared this survey of the foliage immediately surrounding The Grove. Within a native setting of palms, oaks, and magnolias, the blooming plants on the property were deliberately selected for their white blossoms.

During the early 1940s, the construction of a terrace on the east side of the house became a Collins family project. Made of salvaged bricks that had once paved Monroe Street, the terrace became a favorite gathering area that was shady, spacious, and easily accessible to the basement kitchen.

Roy and I always thought of the property surrounding our home as a yard, not a garden. In the early years we were mainly clearing out brambles, weeds, and underbrush. Once we got that under control, we were able to hang swings and hammocks from the trees and have large open spaces for the children to play. We then turned our efforts toward establishing a border of native trees and shrubs that would encompass the property and buffer it from the sounds and sights of the growing Tallahassee community. Oak, magnolia, walnut, pine, and dogwood trees were here when we came, as were Cherokee roses and a variety of palms. Because they grew here naturally, we let them be our guide. Native white flowers, I believe, complement the green foliage here by day and look beautiful in the moonlight as well. For years Gene Ellis, and more recently Mary Doug Buchanan, both professionals and our long time friends, have helped us maintain an atmosphere of informality, spaciousness, simplicity, and privacy—with low maintenance. The yard at The Grove has come a long way since territorial days, yet walking among so many of the same trees and plants makes me feel connected to the past and at peace in the present. It is my favorite place to be.

—Mary Call Collins, 1998

A family cemetery located on the grounds of The Grove is the final resting place for many of those who have lived in and loved the home.

I have fought a good fight,
I have finished my course,
I have kept the faith.
II Timothy 4:7

As the twenty-first century unfolds, The Grove and its grounds maintain a feeling of wilderness as well as a strong sense of place and purpose. Strangely, rather than being anachronistic with the modern city of Tallahassee, the home seems entirely appropriate. It is as though The Grove in all its silence knows that there is a vast difference between being surrounded and being enveloped.

OPPOSITE: **For the Collins family, ringing the "Come Back Bell" at the end of visits is a traditional reminder to children, grandchildren, and great-grandchildren of their constant welcome at The Grove.**

THE GROVE
113

ENDNOTES

RICHARD KEITH AND MARY CALL

1.   Richard Keith Call had two brothers and a sister who survived childhood: George William, a physician who practiced in Kentucky, Missouri, and later in Florida; Jacob, a member of Congress from Missouri; and Mary, "who married Mr. Hawkins of Kentucky." Family Records of Caroline Mays Brevard, p.41 (hereafter CMB Records). These records are part of a larger collection belonging to Mary Call Collins and cited in this book as the Collins Collection.

2.   George Walker served in the state legislature and represented Kentucky in the United States Senate in 1814. David Walker served in the state legislature before representing Kentucky in the United States House of Representatives from 1817 until his death in 1820. David Walker's son of the same name, David S. Walker (Richard Keith Call's first cousin), settled in Leon County in 1837. He served in the Florida Senate from Leon and Wakulla Counties in 1845 (the first legislature

under statehood), and in the Florida House of Representatives from Leon County in 1848. Before becoming Florida's eighth elected governor in 1865, David S. Walker was Florida's Superintendent of Public Instruction, mayor of Tallahassee, and a justice of the Florida Supreme Court. Herbert J. Doherty, *Richard Keith Call, Southern Unionist* (Gainesville, 1961), p. 4; Allen Morris, *The Florida Handbook,* 23rd ed., (Tallahassee, 1991), pp. 325-6.

3.   In 1861, Richard Keith Call began a retrospective journal of his life. He addressed his memories to his first namesake grandson, Richard Call Long, with the hope that the young man might learn from the life of his grandfather. The journal now belongs to the Florida Historical Society and is housed in the Tebeau-Field Library of Florida History in Cocoa. A copy of the original was made available for this book by Mary Call Collins. Journal of Richard Keith Call, p. 6 (hereafter Call Journal).

4.   Richard Keith Call's father and paternal grandfather served in the Revolution-

ary War. His father achieved the rank of colonel in the Continental Army. The uncle for whom he was named (his father's brother, Richard Keith Call) was an original member of the Society of the Cincinnati. Two of his mother's brothers, George and David Walker, were also Revolutionary War veterans (see note 2 above). Doherty, *Richard Keith Call,* p. 5.

5.   Call Journal, p. 7.

6.   Ibid., p. 12; Jackson to Call, November 15, 1821, cited in Sidney Walter Martin, "Richard Keith Call: Florida Territorial Leader," pp. 156-157.

7.   Richard Keith Call received his commission as a first lieutenant in the United States Forty-Fourth Infantry in 1814. Less than a year later, he was promoted to the rank of brevet captain. He was appointed Jackson's second aide-de-camp in 1818. Doherty, *Richard Keith Call,* pp. 8, 10, 12.

8.   Ibid., p. 16.

9. Ibid., p. 22.

10. In Congress, Richard Keith Call was considered an ardent Florida promoter. Though a non-voting territorial delegate, he was credited with strongly influencing the authorization of roads, lighthouses, a navy yard and depot, post offices, and post roads for the new territory. His enthusiasm may also have been a deciding factor in the government's selection of Florida for the Lafayette Land Grant (an 1825 Congressional gift of a land to the Marquis de Lafayette in recognition of his Revolutionary War services). According to Call's biographer, Herbert Doherty, Call was an imperious and commanding man who took his responsibilities seriously and viewed criticism as a challenge to his honor. In 1825, when the newly married Call was considering whether to run for reelection as Florida's territorial delegate to Congress, disparaging comments by political opponents provoked him to give this response: *I am free to admit that I am not calculated for a successful politician so far as success must depend upon a time-serving humiliating policy which would degrade the reputation of a gentleman.—I treat every man with politeness—I am mindful of the rights and interests of all….In serving the Territory, I have made great personal sacrifices. Under these* *circumstances if the people of the territory are disposed to abandon me because I will not lie, fawn, flatter, and deceive—be it so….* Ultimately, Call decided to accept the federally appointed position of Receiver of Public Monies at the land office in Tallahassee and did not seek reelection. Ibid., pp. 35-36, 45; Call Journal, p. 262; Morris, *The Florida Handbook*, p. 369; Doherty, *Richard Keith Call*, pp. 24, 25, 28, 29.

11. Mary Letitia Kirkman (Call) was the daughter of Thomas Kirkman (English) and Ellen Jackson Kirkman (Irish). She was born in Rockfield, Ireland, on July 11, 1801. She moved to America with her family shortly thereafter and was residing in Nashville, Tennessee, by 1809. The future wife of Richard Keith Call had the following brothers and sisters: Thomas, James, Sarah (died in childhood), Jane, Hugh, John, and Alexander. CMB Records.

12. Call Journal, pp. 227-228.

13. Thomas and Ellen Kirkman's disapproval of Andrew Jackson presumably stemmed from Jackson's failure to repay a loan from the Kirkman family. See Andrew Jackson Papers, The Hermitage, Nashville, TN.

14. Andrew Jackson to R. K. Call, November 4, 1821, Call-Brevard Papers, Florida State Archives, Tallahassee.

Theodore Washington Brevard, Sr., Comptroller of the State of Florida, 1853-1861.

15. Mary Letitia Kirkman to Ellen Jackson Kirkman, November 7, 1821, ibid.

16. Ibid.

17. Bernie H. Groene, *Ante Bellum Tallahassee* (Tallahassee, 1971), pp. 18-22.

18. At the time of the May 1825 auction of land outside the city limits of Tallahassee, the southeast quarter and other parcels in Section 25 (the original 640-acres of The Grove property) were patented to Ambrose Crane, publisher of the Tallahassee-based *Florida Intelligencer*, and to Richard Keith Call. The land was immediately adjacent to the northern border of Tallahassee (the southern border of the property was the northern border of the town). Financial difficulty soon caused Crane to leave Tallahassee. With deeds issued on March 15, 1826, all of Section 25 became the property of Richard Keith Call, who was among Ambrose Crane's assignees as his debts were settled. Some maintain that Call obtained the subject property by grant from the federal government. Documentary evidence does not confirm or deny that possibility, but territorial land records indicate that Call's acquisition of the property coincided with the May 1825 auction, suggesting that Call most likely purchased the majority of acreage within Section 25 (excluding Crane's property). This is consistent with property records for other large quantities of land acquired by Call during this time period, which indicates he acquired the property by purchase rather than grant. Groene, *Ante-Bellum Tallahassee*, p. 21; Doherty, *Richard Keith Call,* pp. 44, 50; Leslie Divoll, "The Grove: Historic Structure Part I," p. 15.

19. R. K. Call to Andrew Jackson, September 23, 1825, cited in Doherty, *Richard Keith Call*, p. 43; Call Journal, p. 192.

20. Earliest known use of the name "The Grove" dates to a letter from Mary Call Brevard to her daughter Caroline Brevard (visiting Brevard relatives in North Carolina) in 1891. The reference relates to the whereabouts of Ellen Call Long's widowed daughter, "Nonie" Hollinger. Other references to the home and grounds include: Hickory Grove (1826), The Call Residence (1835), The Mansion House of The State (1860s), Long's Grove (1924), and Grove Hotel (1929, 1934, 1940). Call-Brevard Papers; Divoll, "Historic Structure," p. iii.

21. Author's interview with Mary Call Collins, August 20, 1997.

22. Groene, *Ante-Bellum Tallahassee*, pp. 31-36.

23. Leon County tax roles for 1829 indicate that Richard Keith Call owned 8,754 acres of land, thirteen slaves, town lots

Portrait of Mary Call Brevard, youngest daughter of Richard Keith and Mary Call.

valued at $500, and a four-wheel pleasure carriage. "In little Tallahassee, Call was a big man and only one other person paid more taxes than he did." Doherty, *Richard Keith Call*, p. 57.

24. Under the treaty ceding Florida to the United States in 1821, all grants of Florida land made by Spain after January 24, 1818, were declared and agreed to be null and void. At the time, document tampering and other means of fabricating ownership were complicating land issues in Florida. Given Call's experience with the territorial transfer, he was asked to assist the United States government's efforts to distinguish authentic from fraudulent claims. Ibid., pp. 58-69.

25. When the Florida Legislative Council passed an act to incorporate St. John's Parish on October 30, 1829, Richard Keith Call (a lifelong Episcopalian) was named one of three founding wardens. He provided temporary building space for the town's early Episcopal services and was warden (along with Thomas Eston Randolph) when worship began at St. John's first church building in 1837. Call's commitment to St. John's Church has been faithfully continued by his descendants. Carl Stauffer, *God Willing* (Tallahassee,

Ellen Call Long at home (c. 1890).

1984), pp. 17, 25, 43-44; Doherty, *Richard Keith Call*, p. 57.

26. Call was named president of the Tallahassee Railroad Company in 1834. The line between Tallahassee and St. Marks was one of the first railroads built in Florida. He was an enthusiastic supporter of the railroad because he believed it would increase the value of Florida real estate. The railroad remained one of Call's most important business ventures until 1855, when he sold his stock to the Pensacola and Georgia Railroad. Doherty, *Richard Keith Call*, p. 88; Kate Denison, "Richard Keith Call: Promoter of the Florida Wilderness," p. 37.

27. Call Journal, p. 275.

28. Doherty, *Richard Keith Call*, p. 66.

29. Ellen Call to Mary Call, August 24, 1835, Call-Brevard Papers.

30. According to family lore, while baby Mary Call was at the White House, her bath splashing resulted in a water stain on the ceiling of the Blue Room that was noticeable for years.

31. Mary Kirkman Call to R. K. Call, October 14, 1835, Call-Brevard Papers.

Ellen Call Long on front porch of The Grove with stone tablets salvaged from Fort San Marcos.

32. Ibid.

33. Mary Call to Richard Keith Call, October 27, 1835, ibid.

34. As explained by historian Herbert Doherty, following the United States' acquisition of the Territory of Florida from Spain in 1821, a series of treaties was made between the federal government and the Indian tribes in Florida: Moultrie Creek (1823), which attempted to concentrate the Indian population in the Florida interior; Paynes Landing (1832) and the Additional Treaty (1832), which called for the emigration of Florida Indian tribes to Arkansas (to join Creek Indian territory). The "Additional Treaty" was the treaty signed by several tribal chiefs in support of the emigration plan as defined by the Paynes Landing treaty. Led by Osceola, many Florida Indians were infuriated by the "Additional Treaty" and sought to demonstrate their opposition. Following Senate ratification of the treaty of Paynes Landing and the Additional Treaty in 1834, their resentment burst forth into violence. The protracted conflict that followed (known as the Second Seminole War) lasted until 1842. Doherty, *Richard Keith Call*, pp. 93-98.

35. Doherty, *Richard Keith Call*, p. 98.

36. Family Bibles in the collection belonging to Mary Call Collins record births, deaths, and marriages and include many uncited newspaper articles, notes, and other items regarding such events pertaining to both the Call and Brevard families (hereafter Family Bibles, Collins Collection); Call Journal, p. 287.

37. R. K. Call to John Wyse, August 26, 1836, CMB Records.

38. R. K. Call to Barbara Kirkman, March 3, 1836, Call-Brevard Papers.

39. Ellen Call to R. K. Call, March 25, 1836, cited in Margaret Louise Chapman, Introduction to *Florida Breezes* by Ellen Call Long (Gainesville, 1962), p. ix; Collins Collection.

40. Call Journal, p. 271.

41. R. K. Call to Ellen Kirkman, January 4, 1839, Call-Brevard Papers.

42. Caroline Mays Brevard, "Richard Keith Call," p. 19.

43. Doherty, *Richard Keith Call*, p. 116.

44. Horatio Waldo, "Contemporaneous Pen-pictures of Richard Keith Call and Thomas Brown," pp. 156-157.

45. Groene, *Ante-Bellum Tallahassee,* p. 31.

46. Call pursued a lawsuit during the 1840s which resulted in his obtaining property in the vicinity of Lake Jackson.

Caroline Brevard (c. 1862).

Records also indicate that between 1825 and 1831, Call purchased significant tracts of public lands in Leon County, primarily in the Lake Jackson and Ochlockonee River areas as well as land near the northern limits of Tallahassee. Divoll, "Historic Structure," p. 4; Doherty, *Richard Keith Call,* p. 50.

ELLEN CALL LONG

1. Kate Kirkman to Ellen Call, January 8, 1843, Call-Brevard Papers. Little is known of Ellen Call Long's early childhood. A letter from Andrew Jackson to Richard Keith Call confirms that she and her mother stayed at the Hermitage as guests of the Jacksons in April 1827. During this time, Mary apparently saw her mother (Mary's father died in 1826), and Ellen presumably met her namesake grandmother. Andrew Jackson to R. K. Call, April 23, 1827, ibid.

2. *Weekly True Democrat,* Tallahassee, December 22, 1905; *Tallahassee Democrat,*

December 9, 1976.

3. Over the previous years, the size of the original 640-acre section of property was reduced to 190 acres due to: (1) the court-ordered sale of over one-half of the property (sold in 20-acre parcels) to settle debts incurred as the result of a lawsuit brought against Richard Keith Call and George Walker by Henry Gee and William Bailey in the late 1840s; and (2) the sale of several small parcels in the southeastern corner of the property. Divoll, "Historic Structure," p. 26.

4. In 1850, the Longs operated a farm that produced hay, rye, corn, peas, sweet potatoes, and Irish potatoes. They also kept one hundred hogs, ten cattle, seven horses, and five milk cows. Although discrepancies in census and tax rolls make it impossible to conclude with certainty, The Grove property may have been the location of these activities. It is also possible that before Richard Keith Call moved to his Lake Jackson plantation, the one hundred cattle that he owned in 1848 ranged freely in the wooded property surrounding The Grove. Because the land possibly used for such farming and stock purposes is now heavily developed, physical evidence of the necessary support structures (e.g., a

barn, housing for laborers, etc.) has not been found. A visitor to the area in 1871 published an article in the local paper in which he observed the "very superior" land surrounding The Grove to be in "high cultivation," with a garden close to the home producing "straw-berries, dew-berries, black-berries, raspberries, grapes, figs, peaches, bananas, plums, pears, apples, oranges, lemons, melons, while the fields yield...cotton, sugar, tobacco...." Ibid., p. 27; *Weekly Floridian*, Tallahassee, July 18, 1871.

5. Ellen Call Long to Richard Call Long, August (n.d.), 1853, Call-Brevard Papers.

6. Groene, *Ante-Bellum Tallahassee*, p. 134.

7. Mrs. H. Douglas to Ellen Call Long, August 31, 1853, Call-Brevard Papers.

8. The Brevards were among the early French Huguenots who came to America in 1685. The family settled in North Carolina in the mid-1740s. Captain Alexander Brevard (Theodore, Jr.'s, grandfather) married Rebecca Davidson (daughter of Major John Davidson, of the founding family of Davidson College in North Carolina) in 1784, and soon moved to Lincoln County, North Carolina, and established a home, "Mount Tirzah," near Macpelah. Theodore, Jr.'s, grandfather was an original member of the Society of the Cincinnati; and his great-uncle, Dr. Ephraim Brevard (1750-1783), was the principal author of the Mecklenburg Declaration of Independence, which was adopted one year before the formal Declaration of Independence. Young Theodore's parents, Theodore Washington Brevard (1804-1877) and Caroline Mays Brevard (1811-1892), had one daughter who died in infancy and five sons: Joseph, who died at the age of fourteen; Theodore Washington, Jr., who married Mary Call; Ephraim (1839-1871), a physician who died in an accident at the age of thirty-two; Samuel Mays (1846-1862), who was killed at the age of sixteen while fighting with the Confederate forces in Virginia; and Robert Joseph (1848-1906), who attended Davidson College and later became a prominent North Carolina physician, businessman, and twice elected mayor of Charlotte. Theodore, Sr., and Caroline Brevard moved to Leon County,

Florida, in 1847. Theodore, Sr., served as state Comptroller from 1853-61. Brevard County was named in his honor on January 6, 1855. The couple returned to North Carolina in 1862, where they operated a boarding school in Lincolnton—he taught the boys and she taught the girls. Upon their deaths, they were buried in the family

Theodore Washington Brevard, Jr. (top left), with fellow Confederate soldiers.

Alice Brevard (Gwynn) in 1869.

lot at Macpelah Church. Theodore, Jr., and Mary Call Brevard's children spent a lot of time with their Brevard grandparents and uncle Robert Brevard. CMB Family Records; Morris, *The Florida Handbook*, p. 419; and William L. Sherrill, *The Annals of Lincoln County, North Carolina* (Charlotte, 1937), p. 225.

9. Originally built by Francis Eppes in 1833, the Brevard house no longer stands.

In addition to being a notable Tallahassee resident and community leader, Francis Eppes had the further distinction of being the grandson of Thomas Jefferson. Evelyn Whitfield Henry, "Old Houses of Tallahassee," p. 49.

10. Public records indicate that Medicus Long gave all control and interest in jointly owned property and proceeds from such property to his wife, Ellen Call Long, in 1859. In return for this consideration, he received $5,000. See Divoll, "Historic Structure ," p. 7; Chapman in Long, *Florida Breezes*, p. xi.

11. Divoll, "Historic Structure," p. 10; and Chapman in Long, *Florida Breezes*, p. xi.

12. Groene, *Ante-Bellum Tallahassee*, p. 31; Mary Louise Ellis, William Warren Rogers, and Joan Perry Morris, *Favored Land Tallahassee* (Norfolk, 1988), pp. 36-38.

13. Doherty, *Richard Keith Call*, p. 158.

14. During the Civil War, Richard Call Long served as a courier for General William Miller; Theodore Washington Brevard, Jr., served as an officer and led the 11th Florida Infantry Regiment throughout the siege of Petersburg. Con-

federate President Jefferson Davis promoted Brevard to brigadier general in March 22, 1865 (the war closed before the commission reached him). During the retreat from Petersburg one month later, Brevard was captured and subsequently imprisoned at Johnson's Island, Ohio. His official discharge orders from Johnson's Island dated July 25, 1865, indicate that he was 5' 11" tall, with light skin and hair, and gray eyes. After his release, Brevard returned to his family in Tallahassee, resumed his law practice, and later served two terms in the Florida Senate. On June 20, 1882, Theodore Washington Brevard, Jr., died suddenly of "apoplexy" at the age of forty-six. David J. Coles and Richard J. Ferry, "The Smallest Tadpole: Florida in the Civil War," p. 18; CMB Records.

15. Brevard, "Richard Keith Call," p. 20; Doherty, *Richard Keith Call*, p. 161.

16. Doherty, *Richard Keith Call*, p. 161.

17. Chapman in Long, *Florida Breezes*, pp. xii-xiii.

18. Governor David Shelby Walker's granddaughter, Evelyn Cockrell, claimed that her grandfather lived at The Grove during his term in office (1865-1868).

While no conclusive records have been located, his residency at The Grove is a distinct possibility because there was not an official home for the state executive at that time, and Ellen was offering rooms at her home. Governor Walker was also Ellen's cousin (Richard Keith Call's first cousin). See Call, note 2; Divoll, "Historic Structure," pp. 11, 30.

19. Chapman in Long, *Florida Breezes*, p. xiii.

20. Richard Call Long suffered from an undefined protracted illness before his death on January 10, 1910. At the time of his death, the local paper commented on his "patient endurance of the long years of suffering." Family Bibles, Collins Collection.

21. Chapman in Long, *Florida Breezes*, p. xiii.

22. Ellen Call Long regretfully declined the invitation to join the Historic Mount Vernon Ladies' Association. In her place, she suggested Madam Catherine Murat (great-grand niece of George Washington), who accepted. Years later, Ellen's great-niece Mary Call Collins served the Historic Mount Vernon Ladies' Association as Vice-Regent for Florida from 1961 to 1982. Subsequently, Ellen's great-great-niece Jane Collins Aurell assumed the role in 1985.

23. Chapman in Long, *Florida Breezes*, p. xiv.

24. LeRoy Collins, *Forerunners Courageous* (Tallahassee, 1971), pp. 172-173.

25. As a young girl, Eleanora "Nonie" Long was known for her dark-eyed beauty and free spirit. Personal letters reveal that she had a love for music and travel. Census records indicate that Nonie still considered The Grove her home in 1880. By 1885, she had married Edwin K. Hollinger and moved into her own home. Edwin Hollinger owned and operated a large brick factory on the Ochlockonee River. He was elected to the Florida House of Representatives from Leon County in 1891, but suddenly died the same year leaving Nonie to raise their two sons, E.K. and Robe. Call-Brevard Papers; Divoll, "Historic Structure," p. 11; Records of St. John's Episcopal Church, Tallahassee, FL.

26. Chapman in Long, *Florida Breezes*, p. xxi.

27. The young bride honored by the party was Mrs. Susie Whitfield. Years later, she became the god-mother of Mary Call Collins and shared this memory with her. Author's interview with Mary Call Collins, August 20, 1997.

28. *Weekly True Democrat*, Tallahassee, September 8, 1905.

LeRoy Collins (back row, right) with his Sunday school class in 1914.

29. Chapman in Long, *Florida Breezes*, p. xv.

30. *Weekly Floridian*, Tallahassee, May 26, June 9, and July 28, 1887; Divoll, "Historic Structure," p. 9.

31. In September 1889, Ellen Call Long deeded equal amounts of property to her son and daughter from the land surrounding her home. Her son Richard Long and his family moved into their new home on the property (located at the Northeast corner of Monroe and Georgia Streets) in 1892. Nonie Long Hollinger (who received the land before the death of her husband in 1891) deeded her portion back to her mother 1897. Though the reason remains unconfirmed, Nonie's return of her share of the property may be connected with Ellen's intention to give her The Grove (which would have eliminated the need for Nonie to build another house). Divoll, "Historic Structure," p. 36.

32. Governor William D. Bloxham to Ellen Call Long, March 1899, Call-Brevard Papers.

33. Henry Flagler acquired several other items from Ellen Call Long, both by purchase and gift, including a portrait of

Andrew Jackson and Jackson's field desk. Call-Brevard Papers; Collins, *Forerunners Courageous*, pp. 174-75; Divoll, "Historic Structure," p. 9.

34. The transaction gave Charles Hunt deeds to The Grove and some other property near Lake Jackson. Divoll, "Historic Structure," p. 37.

35. *Weekly True Democrat*, Tallahassee, December 22, 1905.

REINETTE LONG HUNT

1. Reinette's brother, Richard "Dick" Call Long, may have lived with the Hunts in New York for a time. Divoll, "Historic Structure," p. 12.

2. Ellis, Rogers, and Morris, *Favored Land*, p. 92.

3. Divoll reports that after their legal separation in 1907, Charles Hunt reestablished Reinette's legal claim to The Grove and to property near Lake Jackson through new deeds which placed all those lands in trust for Reinette, naming Richard "Dick" Long (Reinette's brother) as trustee. This situa-

Cora Brevard (left) and Mary Call Darby (Collins) with baby cousin John Gywnn in 1920.

tion remained unchanged until 1923, when Reinette received full control over these properties. Divoll, "Historic Structure," p. 39.

4. By the late 1920s, perhaps sooner, Robert Aldridge had a room in The Grove. Upon Reinette's death in 1940, she left him cottages and property that she owned in Panacea (which she rented as a source of occasional income). After LeRoy and Mary Call Collins assumed ownership of The Grove, they found him living in the front end of the basement—his living necessities squeezed tightly between the large barrels comprising his "brewery." As quirky as he was, Robert Aldridge had an indispensable knowledge of the house, and the Collinses offered him a small cottage at the back of the property. He lived there until

Reinette's creative contribution to Tallahassee's Centennial celebration in 1924.

his death in 1951. LeRoy Collins later wrote: "Robert Aldridge, with all his eccentricities and frustrations that followed in his wake, was a good man and a good friend. We could have no doubt of that when we learned first hand of his devotion to The Grove. That something about the house that affected most people whose lives it touched, got to him and held him tightly. The Grove gave something to him and he returned the affection generously and faithfully." Collins, *Forerunners Courageous*, p. 203; Divoll, "Historic Structure," p. 48.

5.   Collins, *Forerunners Courageous*, p. 181

6.   On The Grove property west of the home, a three thousand-seat grandstand was erected for public use during the course of Tallahassee's week long Centennial celebration in 1924. Events held at The Grove included the enactment of two dramas *(Historical Pageant of Tallahassee* and *The Spirit of Freedom)* and a musical gala. Divoll, "Historic Structure," p. 41.

7.   *Florida State Journal,* Tallahassee, November 15, 1924.

8.   Lloyd Logan, "The Call Mansion at Tallahassee, Fla.," p. 13.

9.   Collins, *Forerunners Courageous,* p. 185.

10.   Divoll, "Historic Structure," p. 42.

11.   *Daily Democrat,* Tallahassee, January 2, 1934.

12.   After acquiring the family cemetery in May 1934, the Masons returned it to Mary Call Collins in 1959.

13.   When Reinette died in 1940, she left the real estate comprising The Grove (which she divided into two tracts) to her cousins John Ford and Josephine Agler of Youngstown, Ohio. Ford and Agler were brother and sister and related to Reinette through the Gamble family. The two tracts were again consolidated when LeRoy and Mary Call Collins purchased the property. Divoll, "Historic Structure," pp. 48, 51.

14.   Conceived with the assistance of Reinette's close friend, real estate developer E. N. Brown, the proposed subdivision was

LeRoy Collins, Jr., age two and a half.

to be named "Call Place." Collins, *Forerunners Courageous*, p. 186; Divoll, "Historic Structure," p. 46.

15. Collins, *Forerunners Courageous*, p. 187.

LeRoy and Mary Call Collins

1. In August 1861, Richard Keith Call prepared a will in which he asked that all property previously conveyed to his daughter Ellen Call Long be appraised after his death so that an equal amount could be given to his younger daughter, Mary Call Brevard. The remaining property was then to be further divided equally between the two sisters. The executors of his will (Call's nephew Wilkinson Call and local merchant Thomas Perkins) were involved in the Civil War at the time of Call's death in 1862 and were unable fully to execute his directions. Consequently, the complete appraisal and equal distribution were never formally made. Nonetheless, Mary Call Brevard received a valuable share of her father's Lake Jackson plantation as well as other property located within the city limits of Tallahassee. CMB Records; Divoll, "Historic Structure," 29; Author's interview with Mary Call Collins, January 8, 1998.

2. The Brevards moved into the former Eppes house around 1875. See Long, note 9; Henry, "Old Houses of Tallahassee," p. 49.

3. Described in the local newspaper as "medium sized, black haired, keen eyed, and determined looking," Thomas Arthur Darby was a speculator, a "cotton expert," and a Florida State Senator from Putnam County (26th district, 1895, 1897). CMB Records; Family Bibles, Collins Collection; John B. Phelps, *The People of Lawmaking in Florida 1882-1993* (Tallahassee, 1993).

4. Born on August 29, 1860, Caroline Brevard was the oldest of Theodore and Mary Call Brevard's five children. She never married. A respected teacher, author, and historian, she devoted most of her adult life to education. She wrote several books—the most notable being *Florida History*, which was used in the state's public schools. She taught for many years at Leon High School before joining the faculty at Florida State College for Women, where she taught English and history. Caroline Brevard Elementary School in Tallahassee was named in her honor, as was a dormitory building on the campus of Florida State University. Caroline Brevard was also active in civic, literary, church, and historical organizations including St. John's Episcopal Church, the United Daughters of the Confederacy, and the Colonial Dames. She maintained a keen interest in the efforts of other states regarding the management and use of their historical material, and led a tireless campaign for the establishment of a state department of archives and history in Florida. Caroline Brevard is perhaps most appreciated by succeeding generations of her family for assuming responsibility for the assemblage,

preservation, and maintenance of detailed family records. Call-Brevard Papers; CMB Records; Family Bibles, Collins Collection.

5.   Dr. George Gwynn, Jr., was the only son of Dr. George and Alice Brevard Gwynn. His mother died shortly after his birth in 1892. In 1917, he married Mae Stienman of Baltimore, Maryland, and over the ensuing years they had six children. Another uncle, Richard Call Brevard, also lived at the Monroe Street house. He was a "railroad man" who died at the age of fifty-two on Christmas Day 1913—shortly after Mary Call and Jane Darby's arrival. Family Bibles, Collins Collection.

6.   Family Bibles, Collins Collection.

7.   Author's interview with Mary Call Collins, August 20, 1997.

8.   Of Dr. George and Mae Gwynn's six children, three survived childhood and have remained in Tallahassee: John S. Gwynn, Mae Gwynn Shivers, and Margaret Gwynn Bennett.

9.   Author's interview with Mary Call Collins August 20, 1997.

10.   Nonie Hollinger to Jane Brevard Darby, September 8, 1927, CMB Records.

11.   Collins, *Forerunners Courageous*, p. 189.

12.   LeRoy Collins, The Florida Economic Club, Presentation of Life Service Award (Tallahassee, May 13, 1989).

13.   While he was able to leave home to obtain additional schooling when local options were not available, Collins lamented the fact that others were not as fortunate. The experience motivated him as governor to promote a system of community colleges within driving distance of every Floridian; *Miami Herald*, March 13, 1991.

14.   *Daily Democrat*, Tallahassee, June 10, 1932; Author's interview with Mary Call Collins, September 9, 1997.

LeRoy Collins's parents, Marvin and Mattie Collins, surrounded by family during their fiftieth wedding anniversary celebration at The Grove in 1952.

Collins daughter Mary Call admires family pearls on the eve of her wedding in 1962.

15. Author's interview with Mary Call Collins, September 9, 1997.

16. Ibid.

17. Ibid.

18. Collins, *Forerunners Courageous*, pp. 198-199.

19. Author's interview with Mary Call Collins, September 9, 1997.

20. Ibid.

21. Ibid.

22. Morris, *The Florida Handbook*, pp. 342-343, 608-611.

23. The present site of the Florida Governor's Mansion was part of the original section of land surrounding The Grove. In 1905, the Florida Legislature appropriated $25,000 for the building of an executive residence for the governor on land that was either designated as "public" or made available by private donation. When a "public" site could not be found, George W. Saxon (Tallahassee banker and principal partner of the Tallahassee Land and Improvement Company who bought the property from Ellen Call Long for $10,000 in 1887) donated four lots within the "Long Grove Addition" for the purpose. Dennis Gephardt and Lacy Bullard, *700 North Adams Street*, (Tallahassee,1997) pp. 14, 17.

24. Ibid., pp. 25-29.

25. Educated at Harvard and Yale universities, James Lowry Cogar (1907-1987) taught Social History of the Eighteenth Century at the College of William & Mary in Virginia from 1933-1962. He gained national prominence in the field of historic preservation as the first curator of Colonial Williamsburg from 1931-1948. In addition to his work at Colonial Williamsburg, Cogar served as consultant for many significant preservation projects throughout the country including the restoration of Shakertown at Pleasant Hill, Kentucky. In recognition of his outstanding contributions, the National Trust for Historic Preservation presented him with a Special Award for Significant Achievement in Historic Preservation in the United States in 1971. Charles Dalton Olson, "The Grove: The Role of Interpretation in Creating an Historic House Museum," p. 22.

26. Restoration Architect Joseph Elliot Bright, AIA, received his Bachelor of Architecture degree from the University of Pennsylvania in 1931. A childhood friend of renowned preservationist James Lowry Cogar (see note 25 above), he worked with Cogar at Williamsburg as assistant curator from 1936-1942. From 1949 until his death in 1976, Joseph Bright was an architect in Valdosta, Georgia. Ibid., p. 26.

27. While the Collinses lived at the Governor's Mansion and then in Washington, approximately 10,000 visitors toured the main floor of The Grove during the slightly more than two years it was open as a house museum. Over time, due to the expense of the venture in addition to family needs, the decision was made to stop the tours. Ibid., p. 27; Divoll, "Historic Structure," p. 53.

28. *Time*, December 19, 1955.

29. On May 17, 1954, the United States Supreme court ruled in *Brown vs. Board of Education, Topeka, Kansas*, that segregated school systems were unconstitutional under the fourteenth amendment. In writing the unanimous decision, Chief Justice Earl Warren cited numerous studies demonstrating that "separate school systems were inherently unequal" and detrimentally affected black children. Tom R. Wagy, *Governor LeRoy Collins of Florida: Spokesman of the New South* (University, Alabama, 1985) p. 59.

30. Ibid., p. 61.

31. Historian Tom R. Wagy explains Interposition as a political concept dating back to the late 1700s whereby state authority is interposed between the federal government and the citizens if national officers adopt a position the state considers to be unconstitutional. Wagy further asserts, "The Civil War resolved the dispute over the predominance of federal law, but, for many southerners, the myth of state supremacy remained a cornerstone of their political philosophy. During the 1950s, they again seized upon the concept of interposition as a means to avoid carrying out the Supreme Court's desegregation order." Ibid., p. 63.

President George Bush and Governor and Mrs. Bob Martinez visit with the Collinses at the entrance to The Grove in 1990.

32. LeRoy Collins, May 17, 1954, cited in Wagy, *Governor LeRoy Collins*, pp. 88-89.

33. Ibid., pp 134-136; Tom Fiedler, *Miami Herald*, March 13, 1991.

34. LeRoy Collins, March 20, 1960, cited in Wagy, *Governor LeRoy Collins*, p. 136.

35. John L. Perry, *Tallahassee Democrat*, September 23, 1990.

36. Despite the monetary importance of tobacco advertising to the television medium, Collins was vocal in his disapproval of tobacco advertising aimed at young people. The *New York Times*, reporting on the controversy, quoted Collins as follows:

...if we are honest with ourselves, we cannot ignore the mounting evidence that tobacco provides a serious hazard to health. Can we either in good conscience ignore the fact that progressively more and more of our high-school-age and lower children are now becoming habitual cigarette smokers...? We also know that this condition is being made continually worse under the promotional impact of advertising designed primarily to influence young people.

Certainly the moral responsibility rests first on the tobacco manufacturer. Certainly it also rests on the advertising agencies. Certainly it also rests on the outstanding sports figures who permit their hero status to be prostituted. It is also true that broadcasting and other advertising media cannot be expected to sit in judgment and vouch for the propriety of all advertising presented to the public over their facilities. But where others have permitted their profit motives to subordinate the high purpose of the general good health of our young people, then I think the broadcaster should make corrective moves on his own. This we could do under code amendments, and I feel we should proceed to do so, not because we are required to, but because a sense of moral responsibility demands it.
November 28, 1962.

37. President Lyndon Baines Johnson to

U.S. Attorney General Janet Reno and former state senator Ed Price at The Grove in 1993, following the dedication of the LeRoy Collins Leon County Public Library.

LeRoy Collins, November 8, 1968, Collins Collection.

38. LeRoy Collins to President Lyndon Baines Johnson, November 20, 1968, Ibid.

39. *Tallahassee Democrat*, September 23, 1990; *St. Petersburg Times*, March 13, 1991.

The Architecture

1. Perched atop what has been called the fifth of Tallahassee's seven hills, The Grove occupies an elevation of 204 feet. Jan Pudlow, *Tallahassee Democrat*, January 19, 1997.

2. Federal entries such as the one at The Grove were considered "old fashioned" by the late 1820's. In all probability, these elements were ordered soon after construction started in the mid-1820s. Author's Interview with Professor Manuel Ponce, July 9, 1997.

3. See Collins, notes 25 and 26.

4. *Weekly True Democrat*, Tallahassee, December 4, 1914; *New York Times*, January 24, 1960; Author's interview with Mary Call Collins, September 9, 1997.

5. With discreet floor vents providing air to the main level, ductwork for the system serving the basement and first floor is apparent only at the basement level. Window units provide air conditioning (and reverse-cycle heat) to the second floor. Author's interview with Mary Call Collins, June 30, 1998; Divoll, "Historic Structure," p. 52.

6. Olson, "The Grove," p. 21; Divoll, "Historic Structure," p. 52.

7. Groene, *Ante-Bellum Tallahassee*, p. 31. 1998 population statistic. Tallahassee Area Chamber of Commerce.

The Grove blanketed by snow in 1958.

Identification of Uncaptioned Images

Page 1: Pen and ink rendering of The Grove by artist Ron Yrabedra (1998).

Page 2: LeRoy and Mary Call Collins at home (1980).

Page 4: Theodore Brevard III as a young boy.

Page 8: Mary Call Darby (Collins) shortly before her fourth birthday (1914).

Page 12: Richard Keith Call, Territorial Governor of Florida (1836-1839, 1841-1844).

Page 28: Ellen Call Long (standing) at The Grove with her daughter, Nonie Hollinger (c. 1891).

Page 46: Reinette Long Hunt on the front porch of The Grove with her dog, Diogenes (c. 1920).

Page 56: Mary Call Collins, First Lady of Florida, at The Grove (1956).

Page 92: The front doors of The Grove.

Page 114: Mary Call plunges into her sister Jane's birthday cake at The Grove (1943).

Page 140: "The Grove" as painted by artist Artemis Skevakis Jegart (1952).

BIBLIOGRAPHY

BOOKS & PERIODICALS

Avant, Fenton Garnett Davis. *My Tallahassee.* Edited by David A. Avant, Jr. Tallahassee: L'Avant Studios, 1983.

Chapman, Margaret Louise. Introduction. *Florida Breezes.* By Ellen Call Long. Facsimile repro duction of the 1883 edition. Gainesville: University of Florida Press, 1962. vii-xxiii.

Collins, LeRoy. *Forerunners Courageous: Stories of Frontier Florida.* Tallahassee: Colcade Publishers, Inc., 1971.

Doherty, Herbert J. *Richard Keith Call, Southern Unionist.* Gainesville: University of Florida Press, 1961.

Ellis, Mary Louise; Rogers, William Warren; and Morris, Joan Perry. *Favored Land Tallahassee.* Norfolk: The Donning Company Publishers, 1988.

Gephardt, Dennis and Bullard, Lacy. *700 North Adams Street.* Tallahassee: The Florida Governor's Mansion Foundation, 1997.

Groene, Bertram H. *Ante-Bellum Tallahassee.* Tallahassee: Florida Heritage Foundation, 1971.

Kim's Guide to Florida. Anna Maria: Ethel Byrum Kimball, 1937.

Morris, Allen. *The Florida Handbook.* 23rd ed. Tallahassee: Peninsular Publishing Company, 1991.

Phelps, John B. *The People of Lawmaking in Florida, 1882-1993.* Tallahassee: Florida House of Representatives, 1993.

Sherrill, William L. *The Annals of Lincoln County, North Carolina.* Charlotte: Observer Printing House, Inc., 1937.

Stauffer, Carl. *God Willing: A History of St. John's Episcopal Church, 1829-1979.* Tallahassee: St. John's Episcopal Church, 1984.

Time. December 19, 1955.

Thompson, (James) Maurice. *A Tallahassee Girl.* Boston: Houghton Mifflin, 1881.

Wagy, Thomas R. *Governor LeRoy Collins of Florida: Statesman of the New South.* University: University of Alabama Press, 1985.

COLLECTIONS & MANUSCRIPTS

Andrew Jackson Papers: Collection of letters and other documents. The Hermitage, Nashville, TN.

Call-Brevard Papers: Collection of letters and other documents. Florida Department of State, Bureau of Archives and Records Management, Tallahassee, FL.

Collins Collection: Family Bibles, genealogical records, letters, photographs, and other documents in the private collection of Mary Call Collins, Tallahassee, FL.

Collins, LeRoy. Acceptance Speech. Presentation of Life Service Award, The Florida Economic Club. Tallahassee, May 13, 1989.

Divoll, Leslie. "The Grove: Historic Structure Part I." Unpublished report prepared for the Florida Department of State, 1992.

Journal of Richard Keith Call. Tebeau-Field Library of Florida History, Cocoa, FL.

Photographic Archives. Florida Department of State, Tallahassee, FL.

Records of St. John's Episcopal Church. Tallahassee, FL.

Tallahassee Area Chamber of Commerce. FL.

ARTICLES & THESES

Brevard, Caroline Mays. "Richard Keith Call." *Florida Historical Quarterly,* I (October 1908): 8-20.

Coles, David J. and Ferry, Richard J. "The Smallest Tadpole: Florida in the Civil War." *Military Images* (January-February 1993): 6-31.

Denison, Kate. "Richard Keith Call: Promoter of the Florida Wilderness." *Florida Living* (November 1992): 37.

Henry, Evelyn Whitfield. "Old Houses of Tallahassee." *Tallahassee Historical Society Annual,* I (February 1934): 39-55.

Logan, Lloyd. "The Call Mansion at Tallahassee, Fla." Publication unknown, article located at the Florida State Library, Tallahassee (1914): 13-14.

Martin, Sidney Walter. "Richard Keith Call: Florida Territorial Leader." *Florida Historical Quarterly,* XXI (January 1943): 331-351.

Olson, Charles Dalton. "The Grove: The Role of Interpretation in Creating an Historic House Museum." Unpublished Master's Thesis. Florida Agricultural & Mechanical University, 1995.

Waldo, Horatio. "Contemporaneous Pen-pictures of Richard Keith Call and Thomas Brown." *Florida Historical Quarterly,* VI (January 1928): 156-157.

FILM

Where He Stood. Narrated by Patricia Higgins. WFSU-TV, Tallahassee. September 1990.

NEWSPAPERS

Daily Democrat, Tallahassee, 1932, 1934, 1940.
Florida Sentinel, Tallahassee, 1862.
Florida State Journal, Tallahassee, 1924.
Floridian, Tallahassee, 1836.
Miami Daily News, 1954.
Miami Herald, 1954, 1970, 1989-1991, 1995.
New York Times, 1960, 1962.
Orlando Sentinel, 1954.
Panama City News Herald, 1965.
St. Petersburg Times, 1960, 1991.
Tallahassee Democrat, 1942, 1959, 1965, 1974, 1976-1977, 1979, 1985, 1990-1991, 1997.
Tampa Tribune, 1956, 1988.
Weekly Floridian, Tallahassee, 1871, 1887.
Weekly True Democrat, Tallahassee, 1905, 1907, 1914.

PHOTO & ILLUSTRATION CREDITS

With Ray Stanyard as principal photographer, the design of this book is the work of Denise Choppin. Some of the photographs that are credited to the personal collection of the Collins family are also available at the Florida State Archives. Listed below are the public and private collections generously made available to the author for the purpose of this publication. In addition, the talents of the following skilled professionals have greatly enhanced the final product:

COLLECTIONS

Collins Family Collection

Florida State Archives

Florida State Library

Courtesy of Mr. and Mrs. John S. Gwynn

Courtesy of Mr. and Mrs. Frank Shaw, Jr.

ILLUSTRATIONS

John S. Hand, Architect

Patrick Hodges, Landscape Architect

Artemis Skevakis Jegart, Artist

Peter Krafft, Cartographer

Charles D. Olson, Architectural Designer

Ron Yrabedra, Artist

PHOTOGRAPHY *(ALL RIGHTS RESERVED)*

Mickey Adair, Available Light Photography

Fabian Bachrach, Photographer

Michael Burchfield, Photographer

William Carnes, Photographer

Beverly Frick, Photographer

Lois Griffin, Griffin Gallery of Fine Photography

Russell Photography

Harvey Slade, Photographer

Ray Stanyard, Stanyard Photography

Cover: *(front)* photography by Ray Stanyard

Endpaper: John S. Hand

1: drawing by Ron Yrabedra

2: photography by Beverly Frick

4: Florida State Archives

8: Collins Family Collection

10-11: Collins Family Collection

12: Collins Family Collection, photography by Ray Stanyard

15: Florida State Library

17: courtesy of Mr. and Mrs. John S. Gywnn, photography by Ray Stanyard

19: Florida State Archives

20: *(left)* Florida State Archives; *(right)* Collins Family Collection, photography by Ray Stanyard

23: photography by Ray Stanyard

24: Collins Family Collection, photography by Ray Stanyard

26: Florida State Archives

27: *(left)* Florida State Archives; *(right)* Collins Family Collection, photography by Ray Stanyard

28: Florida State Archives

30: Collins Family Collection, photography by Ray Stanyard

31: Collins Family Collection, photography by Ray Stanyard

32: Collins Family Collection, photography by Ray Stanyard

33: Collins Family Collection, photography by Ray Stanyard

35: *(top left)* Florida State Archives; *(bottom left)* Collins Family Collection, photography by Ray Stanyard

36: Collins Family Collection

37: Florida State Archives

38: Collins Family Collection, photography by Ray Stanyard

39: Collins Family Collection, photography by Ray Stanyard

40: Florida State Archives

42: Florida State Archives

44: Florida State Archives

45: Florida State Archives

46: Collins Family Collection

48: Florida State Archives

50: Collins Family Collection, photography by Ray Stanyard

51: *(left)* Collins Family Collection, photography by Ray Stanyard; *(right)* Collins Family Collection

52: photography by Ray Stanyard

54: Florida State Library

55: Florida State Archives

56: Florida State Archives

58: *(top)* Collins Family Collection, photography by Ray Stanyard; *(bottom)* Collins Family Collection

59: *(left)* Collins Family Collection; *(right)* Collins Family Collection, photography by Ray Stanyard

60: Collins Family Collection

61: *(top)* Collins Family Collection; *(bottom right)* Collins Family Collection, photography by Ray Stanyard

62: Collins Family Collection

63: Collins Family Collection

65: Collins Family Collection

66: Collins Family Collection

68: Collins Family Collection

69: Florida State Archives

70: Collins Family Collection

71: Collins Family Collection

72: Collins Family Collection

73: Collins Family Collection

74: Collins Family Collection

75: Collins Family Collection

76: *(top left and center)* Florida State Archives; *(bottom right)* photography by Fabian Bachrach

77: Collins Family Collection

79: *(top)* Time / Collins Family Collection, photography by Ray Stanyard; *(bottom)* Collins Family Collection

80: *(top)* Collins Family Collection; *(bottom right)* Collins Family Collection, photography by Ray Stanyard

81: Collins Family Collection

82: *(top left)* photography by William Carnes; *(top and bottom right)* photography by Harvey Slade; *(center)* Collins Family Collection, photography by Ray Stanyard

84: Collins Family Collection

85: Collins Family Collection

86: *(top left and right)* Collins Family Collection; *(bottom left)* photography by Ray Stanyard

87: *(top)* photography by Mickey Adair; *(bottom)* photography by Ray Stanyard

89: photography by Beverly Frick

90: *(left)* photography by Harvey Slade; *(top and bottom right)* photography by Lois Griffin

91: *(left)* photography by Michael Burchfield; *(right)* photography by Beverly Frick

92: photography by Ray Stanyard

94: architectural rendering by Charles D. Olson, lettering by John S. Hand, photography by Ray Stanyard

97: photography by Ray Stanyard

98: photography by Ray Stanyard

99: photography by Ray Stanyard

100: photography by Ray Stanyard

101: photography by Ray Stanyard

102: *(left)* photography by Ray Stanyard; *(bottom right)* Collins Family Collection, photography by Ray Stanyard

103: photography by Ray Stanyard

104: photography by Ray Stanyard

105: photography by Ray Stanyard

106: map by Peter Krafft

107: survey by Patrick Hodges

108: photography by Ray Stanyard

109: photography by Ray Stanyard

110: photography by Ray Stanyard

111: photography by Ray Stanyard

112: photography by Ray Stanyard

113: photography by Ray Stanyard

114: Collins Family Collection

116: Collins Family Collection

117: Collins Family Collection

118: Collins Family Collection

119: Collins Family Collection

120: Collins Family Collection, photography by Ray Stanyard

121: Collins Family Collection, photography by Ray Stanyard

122: Florida State Archives

123: Collins Family Collection

124: Collins Family Collection

125: Collins Family Collection

126: Collins Family Collection

127: Collins Family Collection

128: photography by Harvey Slade

129: Collins Family Collection

130: Collins Family Collection

131: Collins Family Collection

138: *(center)* Collins Family Collection; *(right)* photography by Michael Burchfield

139: *(left)* Collins Family Collection; *(top right)* photography by Russell; *(bottom right)* Collins Family Collection

140: painting by Artemis Skevakis Jegart, courtesy of Mr. and Mrs. Frank Shaw, Jr., photography by Ray Stanyard

142: Collins Family Collection

Flyleaf: photography by Beverly Frick

Cover: *(back)* photography by Ray Stanyard

Color separations, scanning, and placement by Lithohaus Printers, Inc., Tallahassee, Florida.

THE FAMILY OF
LeRoy & Mary Call Collins

LeRoy Collins, Jr. (b. 1934)
m. Carol Jane Sisson (b. 1934)

— Carol Jane Collins (b. 1961)
   m. David Gregory Smith (b. 1959)
      Virginia Darby Smith (b. 1992)
      Gregory Coyle Smith (b. 1994)
      Hannah Collins Smith (b. 1998)
      Katherine Grace Smith (b. 1998)

— Helen Call Collins (b. 1963)
   m. (1) Michael Phillip Jacob (b. 1957)
      Phillip Call Jacob (b. 1990)
   m. (2) Victor Doroteo Ines (b. 1945)
      Christian Alexander Ines (b. 1995)
      Sara Irene Ines (b. 1997)

— LeRoy Collins III (b. 1966)

— Edward Sisson Collins (b. 1973)
   m. Janinne Marie Hoffman (b. 1972)
      Ayden Elizabeth Collins (b. 1998)

Jane Brevard Collins (b. 1938)
m. John Karl Aurell (b. 1935)

— Jane Brevard Aurell (b. 1964)
   m. John Stephen Menton (b. 1955)
      Jane Darby Menton (b. 1993)
      Caroline Brevard Menton (b. 1997)

Sarah Darby Collins (b. 1950)
m. Frederick Douglas Begeman (b. 1943)

— Frederick Douglas Begeman, Jr. (b. 1977)

— Christopher Collins Begeman (b. 1980)

— John Brevard Begeman (b. 1982)

Mary Call Collins (b. 1942)
m. Henry Palmer Proctor (b. 1941)

— Mary Call Proctor (b. 1965)
   m. Roy Molitor Ford, Jr. (b. 1965)
     Roy Molitor Ford III (b. 1995)
     Proctor Kirkman Ford (b. 1996)

— Henry Palmer Proctor, Jr. (b. 1967)

— LeRoy Collins Proctor (b. 1969)
   m. Kathryn Anne Shasteen (b. 1970)

— Sarah Ball Proctor (b. 1977)

BENEFACTORS

Knight Ridder

The Miami Herald

Ausley & McMullen

Rutledge, Ecenia, Underwood, Purnell & Hoffman, P.A.

Tours with a Southern Accent

Richard L. and Joan Wadsworth West

Mr. and Mrs. Eugene C. Patterson

Richard and Betty Higginbotham

Mr. James Elliott Messer and Family

Mr. and Mrs. Wilfred C. Varn

Mrs. Alice C. Wadsworth

Mr. and Mrs. Murray M. Wadsworth

Mr. and Mrs. John C. Menton

Mr. and Mrs. John K. Aurell

The Collins Family

The text was set in Garamond
with decorative capitals
in Perpetua Titling.
Black and white archival
photographs were scanned in
full color and tonally enhanced.
Printing was done on a
Komori Lithrone 440
in process color
on Potlatch McCoy
100 pound text, silk finish.

The
Call-Collins
Family

Richard Keith Call
1792 - 1862

Medicus Long   Ellen Walker Call
1816 -   1825 - 1905

Richard Call Long   Cora Gamble
1846 - 1910   1850 - 1936

Richard Call Long, Jr.   Charles Edwin Hunt   Reinette Gamble Long
1883 - c. 1935   1873 - 1940

Caroline Mays Brevard   Richard Call Brevard   Thomas Arthur Darby   Jane Kirkman Bre
1860 - 1920   1861 - 1913   1857 - 1923   1868 - 1932

Thomas LeRoy Collins   Mary Call Darby
1909 - 1991   1911 -

Le Roy Collins, Jr.   Jane Brevard Col
1934 -   1938 -